THE PRICE MECHANISM
AND THE MEANING
OF NATIONAL
INCOME STATISTICS

The Price Mechanism
and the Meaning of
National Income Statistics

by

DAN USHER

CLARENDON PRESS OXFORD
1968

Oxford University Press, Ely House, London W. 1

GLASGOW NEW YORK TORONTO MELBOURNE WELLINGTON
CAPE TOWN SALISBURY IBADAN NAIROBI LUSAKA ADDIS ABABA
BOMBAY CALCUTTA MADRAS KARACHI LAHORE DACCA
KUALA LUMPUR HONG KONG TOKYO

PRINTED IN GREAT BRITAIN
BY THE UNIVERSITY PRESS
ABERDEEN

To Samphan

W. L. F. D. C. H.

Acknowledgements

M OST of the research for this book and the preparation of the first draft were done while I was a research fellow at Nuffield College, Oxford. My first studies of national income were conducted during my tenure as a Hallsworth Fellow in economics at the University of Manchester. I am enormously grateful for these fellowships. But for them, it is unlikely that this book would have been written. The Rockefeller Foundation financed a period of study in Thailand and the Bank of Thailand provided facilities for research. The Graduate School of Business of Columbia University and Queen's University supported my research at a later stage.

I am pleased to acknowledge my appreciation for assistance from Mr. Prakorb Juangbhanich of the Thai National Income Office; Mr. Peter Gajewski of the United States Operations Mission to Thailand; Mr. Manas Ratanaruk, Mr. Phut Hotrabhavanond, and Mr. Vera Natalang of the Thai Ministry of Economic Affairs; Mrs. Soparb Yossundara, Mr. Subhjai Sri-Kasibandhu, and Mr. Thawai Choeyklin of the Bank of Thailand; Dr. M. Wagner of Kasetsart University in Bangkok; Mrs. Chamchitta Loahavadhana of the Siam Commercial Bank in Chiengmai and Mr. Pramote Songchaikul of the Bangkok Bank Ltd. Professor B. Yamey's comments and suggestions on my papers in *Economica* resulted in improvements that are reflected in this book. His editorial modesty prevented me from acknowledging his help at the time and I am pleased to do so now. Professor S. Kuznets has been kind enough to read an early draft of the book and the present version has benefited from his suggestions. I particularly appreciate the advice and encouragement of Professor P. T. Bauer of the London School of Economics and of Professor S. H. Frankel of Nuffield College, Oxford. My sister-in-law, Mrs. Sarah Usher, edited part of the manuscript and improved the style considerably. My wife Samphan helped out in many ways, as translator, statistician, typist, and diplomat.

Permission has been kindly granted by the London School of Economics and Political Science to reproduce parts of 'The Transport Bias in Comparisons of National Income', 'Equalizing Differences in Income and the Interpretation of National Income Statistics', and 'Income as a Measure of Productivity', articles that appeared in *Economica* in May 1963, August 1965, and

November 1966 respectively; by the Institute of Economic Affairs to reproduce portions of *Rich and Poor Countries, A Study in Problems of Comparisons of Real Income*; and by the University Press of the Australian National University to reproduce portions of 'The Thai Rice Trade', a chapter in *Thailand: Social and Economic Studies in Development* edited by Professor T. Silcock.

DAN USHER

Queen's University
Kingston
November 1967

Contents

Introduction and Summary

My interest in the meaning of national income statistics began when I was working with the United Nations in Bangkok. In Thailand I saw a people not prosperous by European standards but obviously enjoying a standard of living well above the bare requirements of subsistence. Many village communities seemed to have attained a standard of material comfort at least as high as that of slum dwellers in England or America. But at my desk I computed statistics of real national income showing people of underdeveloped countries including Thailand to be desperately if not impossibly poor. The contrast between what I saw and what I measured was so great that I came to believe that there must be some large and fundamental bias in the way income statistics are compiled.

The statistics so at variance with appearances were of national income per head in $U.S., constructed by dividing the total national income in local currency by the product of the population and the foreign exchange rate between the local currency and $U.S.[1] A few examples are shown in Table 1.

Something is very wrong with these statistics. For instance, if the figure of $40 for Ethiopia means what it appears to mean, namely that Ethiopians are consuming per year an amount of goods and services no larger than could be bought in the United States for $40, then most Ethiopians are so poor that they could not possibly survive, let alone increase their numbers. If the $40 does not refer to the amount of goods and services that could be bought in the United States for $40, then it is not clear what it does refer to or if it refers to anything at all. It is curious that statistics as ambiguous as these are quoted so frequently.

---

[1] In 1963 the national income of India was 163 thousand million rupees, the population was 451 million, and the foreign exchange rate was 4·76 rupees to the dollar. The national income per head in $U.S. was therefore $76 (163 ÷ (4·76 × 0·451)).

Perhaps familiarity with these statistics has made them acceptable. Perhaps it is felt that statistics showing the inhabitants of poor countries to be poorer than anyone could possibly be, must indicate that these people are very poor indeed. For many countries, there are no other statistics of comparative national income, and it is believed with some justification that these statistics order countries more or less correctly on the scale of rich and poor.

TABLE I

Estimates of Gross Domestic Product in $U.S. per Head in 1963

United States	2790	Rhodesia	139
France	1406	Thailand	101
United Kingdom	1361	India	76
Argentina	563	Burma	64
Turkey	230	Ethiopia	40

Source: *Yearbook of National Accounts Statistics 1964.* United Nations, Table 6A.

There are, however, several reasons for delving more deeply into the matter: (a) One would like to have measures of the degree of poverty or prosperity of countries that make physiological and economic sense. (b) One cannot be sure that the U.N. figures order real national incomes correctly unless one understands why the absolute magnitudes are incorrect. (c) There are strong economic reasons associated with the purchasing power parity doctrine for believing that the method of comparing real national incomes used by the U.N. ought to yield the right results. It is worth finding out why economic theory leads us astray and how the error can be rectified. (d) It is important to know how deep the error goes into national income analysis. Statistics of incomes of regions in a single country have much in common with the U.N. statistics of real national incomes of countries. Are incomes of regions within a country free of whatever it is that is biasing down incomes of some countries? To go one step further, statistics of income per man employed, as measures of productivity of industries, have much in common with statistics of incomes of regions, especially when each industry tends to be concentrated in a region. Are productivity statistics biased also? The answer to both of these questions is yes. The forces that bias down the national incomes in $U.S. of the underdevelpəd ocountries may also affect incomes of regions within a country and the statistics of productivity. The demonstration of the truth of this proposition and the analysis of how the price mechanism plays tricks with the national income statistics are the main themes of this book. The book is organized around three questions, each of which is the subject of one of the three parts of the book. The questions are:

1. What is real income?
2. Why do the statistics we use to measure real income signify something other than what we intend?
3. What is the order of magnitude of the discrepancy?

The first part of the book is an examination of the concept of real income with special reference to comparisons among rich and poor countries. It is also a how-to-do-it guide, for the meaning of real income is not firmly pinned down until it can serve as a blueprint to the statistician. Part of the problem is to decide what is income and what is not. Under the general heading of 'inclusion or exclusion' fall such questions as: Is transport to work in one's own car a final product or an intermediate product? The fact that this item is paid for by the consumer would seem to justify designating it as a final product and including it in income. But the fact that transport to work yields no benefit in itself and is a social cost of producing goods and services already included in the accounts would seem to imply that transport to work should be classified as intermediate and excluded from the national income. Should home-grown food be counted as part of income? What of the village barber or the services of the mayor or village entertainment? Should heating cost be included in income in a comparison between a cold country where heating is required and a hot country where it is not? Questions of this sort were posed when national income estimates were first being prepared, and answers to them are implicit in the practice of each national income office. Answers appropriate for the compilation of income figures in a single country are not necessarily appropriate for international comparison.

Once it is decided what items income is to contain, it is necessary to choose a set of price weights so that goods in different countries may be compared on the same scale. This is an index number problem, but unlike some index number problems, it may have a unique solution. There may be a single correct way to choose price weights in an income comparison. An exact and correct ratio of real incomes in two situations can be found when one is quite clear about the meaning to be attributed to the phrase 'real income'. For instance, in a comparison between England and Thailand, the real income per head in Thailand might be the amount of money a typical Englishman would require in England to be as well off as he would be in Thailand with an average income there. This specification of the meaning of real income implies an exact ratio of the real incomes of Thailand and England, a ratio that may be aimed at in designing statistics. A similar test on a typical Thai would give rise to a ratio of Thai and English incomes as seen by Thai standards. The two ratios differ. The reason why they differ is not that one real income can be measured in several ways, but that real income is a generic term referring collectively to the answers to a number of questions that are similar but not identical. In principle, each question admits an exact answer.

In practice, when a statistician is told to compute estimates of real income, he is not given a single precise question to answer, and even if he were he would not have enough information to answer it accurately. Under these circumstances, it is often best to follow a conventional rule of thumb, which is to take two ratios of income, one at each country's prices, and to suppose the ratio one is looking for lies in between them.

So much attention has been given in the economic literature to the index number problem that one might suppose the choice of prices to be the only substantial issue in income comparison. In fact there is as much of a problem in the choice of commodities. Imagine a comparison between a tropical and a temperate country. The item 'fruit' could be dealt with either by treating all fruit as a single commodity measured in pounds, or by treating varieties separately. If mangoes, papayas, lychees, apples, pears, grapes, etc., appear as separate commodities in the comparison, then income associated with the consumption of fruit in each country will be very large when fruit is valued at the other country's prices and very small when fruit is valued at its own prices, for tropical fruit is expensive in temperate countries and fruit native to temperate countries is expensive in tropical countries. In general, the finer the breakdown of commodities in an income comparison, the better off each country appears at the other country's prices and the wider the gap between ratios of income valued at the two sets of prices. Either country can be made to look more prosperous if the commodities in its national income are specified in detail while commodities in the other country's national income are not.

The second and most important of the three main parts of the book is an attempt to explain the 'impossibly' low national income figures of the underdeveloped countries in $U.S. per head by the operation of the international price mechanism. It will be shown how the international price mechanism can divest a figure like $40 per head, as the national income of Ethiopia, of its 'obvious' welfare interpretation, namely that Ethiopians are no better off than Americans would be if they had only $40 to spend over a year, and cause it to mean something altogether different.

The principal cause of the anomalous statistics in Table 1 is that price levels are very low in poor countries; price levels in underdeveloped areas of as little as a third or a quarter of price levels in the United States are not atypical. A country may have a low national income per head in $U.S. because its real income is low or because its price level, converted to $U.S., is low. Generally the two causes reinforce each other; price levels tend to be low in poor countries and high in rich countries. The connection between low price levels and poor countries is not a consequence of balance of payments difficulties or of pegging of artificial exchange rates, though the latter is sometimes important. Low price levels in the underdeveloped countries are not indicative of a disequilibrium in international trade but are consistent with fluctuating exchange rates and with balanced trade.

Characterization of price levels in countries as high or low may seem strange at first because each country has its own currency, and price levels in countries with different currencies are not comparable until the currencies are converted to a common unit. Much of the theory developed in Part II pertains to a world in which one currency is used everywhere, as if the gold standard were still in force. In the nineteenth century it would have been possible to characterize price levels as high or low in terms of gold. The same ranking of price levels and national incomes could be obtained in a world of paper currencies and fluctuating exchange rates if all incomes were converted to the same common currency unit by the foreign exchange rate. Arbitrage would force the two systems of measurement to yield the same results. Price levels can even be designated as high or low when foreign exchange rates are fixed by national governments, as long as rates are chosen to balance payments in foreign trade. Under present international financial arrangements, with some exchange rates too high and others too low, the pattern of real national incomes got by converting all currencies into $U.S. deviates somewhat from the pattern that would emerge if there were a world currency and all national incomes were expressed in that currency. But as a rule the deviation between actual exchange rates and equilibrium exchange rates is small by comparison with the differences in equilibrium price levels. Where this is not so, corrections have to be made to the exchange rate before the type of analysis examined in this book can be attempted.

Four main forces are identified as causing price levels to differ from place to place: the pricing of products that do not enter into international trade, asymmetrical international transport cost, asymmetrical domestic transport cost, and trade taxes. A chapter is devoted to each, and it is shown how each force, alone or in combination with others, could depress price levels in poor countries.

The pricing of products that do not enter into international trade

Economic progress enables men to make goods with less expenditure of labour. It has less effect on the provision of services. Rich countries are rich because they have more things, more cars, more radios, more clothing, more food. Rich countries are relatively less well-provided in services, in civil servants, policemen, domestic servants, retail traders, barbers, and teachers. Since goods enter international trade, while services as a rule do not, an international trade causes prices of goods to be more or less the same everywhere (this is the rationale of the purchasing power parity doctrine), but services are relatively cheap in poor countries where they are abundant, and expensive in rich countries where they are scarce. Consequently national incomes of rich countries are high because rich countries consume more goods, and because rich countries put high prices on services. The first reason corresponds to a genuinely higher standard of living; the second does not.

International transport cost

A country's price level may be forced down by the transport cost of the products it exports. Transport cost causes Thai exports to be cheaper in Thailand than in the U.K. and U.K. exports to be cheaper in the U.K. than in Thailand. However, the effects of transport costs on price levels need not cancel out completely. The Thai price level may be lowered relative to the U.K. price level if exports from the U.K. to Thailand are primary products or semi-finished products that are ultimately re-exported from Thailand to the U.K. (Thailand sells rice to the U.K. in exchange for fertilizer), if Thai exports require greater transport costs than do the exports of the U.K., or if the Thai exports are commodities that enter in an important way into the cost of living while the U.K. exports do not (Thailand sells rice to the U.K. in exchange for heavy machinery).

Domestic transport cost

Just as international transport cost can affect price levels in different parts of the world, so domestic transport cost can affect price levels in different parts of a country. Suppose international trade between Thailand and the U.K. takes place in the first instance between their capital cities and that price levels are the same in the two capital cities. The price level in Thailand as a whole may still be less than the price level in the U.K. as a whole if prices in the Thai hinterland are held down by the high cost of transporting goods from the hinterland to the capital city.

Trade taxes

There is a well-known symmetry among import taxes, export taxes, export subsidies, and import subsidies; each pair of taxes inhibits trade and each pair of subsidies promotes trade. A second symmetry among trade taxes pairs off the four differently. Import taxes and export subsidies tend to raise the domestic price level, and to increase money income at world prices. Export taxes and import subsidies tend to lower the domestic price level and to decrease the money national income, even though the real national income is unchanged. In their effect on income, trade taxes and subsidies are like transport cost; an import tax is like international transport cost on imports; an export subsidy is like negative transport cost on exports, etc.

Comparison of real national income is studied in this book within the confines of traditional economic analysis, in the sense that men are presumed to maximize utility subject to constraints. The analysis differs from the main body of economics in some of the assumptions about the economic environment. In particular, the subject matter of this investigation forces one to take geography seriously. Ordinary economic analysis, other than location theory, attaches a unique price to each commodity, as if the economy were condensed into a single location or a single point in space. A study of the influence of the price mechanism on income comparison must be conducted in a framework that allows prices of identical goods or services to differ from place to place, for this difference is the thing to be explained. Part of the analysis is conducted in the two-point world used extensively in the theory of international trade. But the chapter on domestic transport cost makes use of a genuine two-dimensional geography in the form of a disc-shaped country like Von Thunen's isolated state.

The theory developed in Part II cuts across the division between micro-economics and macro-economics. Micro-economics is the study of the formation of relative prices. Macro-economics is the study of the main aggregates of national income on the assumption that prices are set in advance. Professor Hicks has recently called attention to the distinction between 'fixprice' and 'flexprice' methods in economics, the former having national income analysis and macro-economics as its domain, and the latter having micro-economics as its domain. A novel feature of Part II, the feature that gives this book its title, is that flexprice methods are introduced into the study of the national accounts. To understand the meaning of national income statistics, it is necessary to consider how relative prices are determined. Each of the four forces that may depress price levels in poor countries is associated with the way relative prices are formed, and the working of these forces cannot be observed until fixprice methods are abandoned in favour of flexprice methods. This way of looking at national income statistics identifies problems that were hitherto not seen as problems at all. Once it is recognized that national income statistics are not necessarily indicators of welfare it becomes clear that income statistics of all kinds may fail to carry the social implications required of them. It has already been mentioned that statistics of income per head by provinces may not show which provinces are the most prosperous because price levels may differ among provinces. Lorenz curves or Gini coefficients alleged to show the distribution of real income may be seriously misleading if rich people (or poor people) tend to congregate in high price areas. The chapter on domestic transport cost contains a model in which the productivity statistics, income per man employed by industry, are completely misleading because farmers live in low price areas. The difficulty is not that the statistics are wrong; it is that they mean something other than what they are usually believed to mean.

A rule is needed for deciding when incomes should be compared in real terms and when they should be compared in money terms. The distinction between comparison of incomes in money terms and in real terms turns on whether income statistics are corrected for price levels. A ratio of incomes of France and Germany at German prices, and an estimate of rate of growth of the American income valued at 1958 prices, are examples of income comparison in real terms. Productivity statistics and Gini coefficients are examples of comparison in money terms. A reasonable criterion for deciding which type of comparison to use is that the statistics should reflect what is maximized. When men maximize money income, the statistics should compare money income. When men maximize real income, the statistics should compare real income.

The statistical problem of how to compare incomes leads to the theoretical problem of deciding when men maximize real income and when they maximize money. It turns out that in deploying his resources in circumstances where prices and price levels vary from place to place, economic man sometimes maximizes money income and sometimes maximizes real income, real income being money income weighted by a local price index. As a first approximation it might be said that labour maximizes real income and capital maximizes money income. Labour maximizes real income because the labourer must reside and spend most of his income in the place where it is earned. Capital maximizes money income because the owner of capital is free to live away from his possessions and is therefore indifferent to the price level at the place where his capital is employed. This result is at variance with the almost universal belief among economic theorists that maximization of money income is the only valid criterion.

The connection between the theory and the underdeveloped countries is one of degree rather than of kind. A rough empirical judgement is made that the net effect of the four forces biasing income comparisons is to make the poor countries appear poorer than they are. There are exceptions, and instances can be found where some of the forces work in the opposite direction. Furthermore, all the forces causing prices of identical products to differ between rich and poor countries have their counterparts between two rich countries or two poor countries. The emphasis is on the contrast between rich and poor countries because this is the context in which the problem arose and because the tendency of the biases in income measurement to be especially large in this context enables us to obtain a clear view of the forces at work. It is sometimes said that economic theory applies more nearly to developed than to underdeveloped countries. This is an instance of the reverse. The relatively simple economies of the underdeveloped countries and the great contrast between developed and underdeveloped countries permit us to see an aspect of everyday economic life in an extrapolated and magnified form.

The third and final part of this study is an application of these ideas to the interpretation of the national income of Thailand and an attempt to quantify the forces and biases examined in Part II. Considerations of time limited the study to a single country and the interests of the author determined which country that would be. Thailand has an advantage as an object for this study in that the contrast between the appearance of prosperity and the measure of real income is particularly striking, but there are other countries that would have done as well. Three distinct but related subjects are treated in separate chapters; these are the comparison of real income between Thailand and the U.K., the source of price differentials in traded goods between these countries, and the interpretation of the Thai productivity statistics.

The ratio of the U.K. national income per head to the Thai

national income per head when both incomes are converted into a common currency by the foreign exchange rate, is shown in Table 1 to be thirteen to one. This is the most commonly-used statement of comparative real incomes. A different picture emerges when real incomes are compared by weighting quantities consumed in each country by a common set of prices. At Thai prices, the ratio of real incomes is about six and a half to one; at U.K. prices it is only two and a half to one. Thailand appears better off when both national incomes are evaluated at U.K. prices than when they are evaluated at Thai prices. Thailand also appears substantially better off at either its own prices or U.K. prices than it does when all incomes are converted to dollars through the foreign exchange rate. The first of these statements is in accordance with a general proposition that may be found in any textbook of economics. The second is explained by the theory developed in Part II. Averaging the ratios of U.K. real income to Thai real income at Thai and U.K. prices yields a new ratio of about four to one and an implicit ratio of U.K. to Thai price levels of about three to one. Relative prices of services—public administration, legal, religious, medical, educational, and domestic—cluster around ten to one. All of these numbers must be taken with a grain of salt. They represent my view of a reasonable estimate of comparative welfare. I had to make a number of fairly arbitrary decisions about how to manipulate the data, and another statistician may have done this differently.

Though the largest of the price differentials between Thailand and the U.K. are on items that do not enter into international trade, price differentials on traded commodities appear disconcertingly high. The differential on rice, for instance, is 359 per cent of the Thai price. An attempt is made to trace the price of rice through all stages of distribution from the farm in Thailand to the consumer in the U.K. The total differential is divided into distribution in Thailand, milling, export, and distribution in the U.K., and this information is used to gain insight into the relative strength of the forces biasing down price levels in poor countries. This investigation was limited to one commodity because of the time it takes to collect the required information, and rice was chosen because it is by almost any standard the most important commodity in the Thai economy. An interesting fact that comes out of this study is that about half the price differential is due to distribution cost in the U.K. and that the U.K. distribution cost is about ten times the Thai distribution cost. All goods purchased retail may be thought of as 'joint products' of production and distribution, distribution being a service that does not enter into international trade. Thus the tendency for services not entering into international trade to be cheap in poor countries, lowers the price not only of pure services like public administration and education but also of goods, by means of their 'service' component.

Biases in comparisons of real incomes among nations have their counterparts in all kinds of income comparisons—comparisons of productivity among industries, of real incomes among states, and of the shares of income of social classes. Productivity statistics are taken as an example. When computed in the usual way, the productivity of labour in Thai agriculture appears to be a tenth of the productivity of labour in other sections of the Thai economy. Corrections for differences in the cost of living on the farms and in the city, for the effects of trade taxes, and for certain other biases in measurement, increase the productivity of agriculture relative to the productivity of other sectors from a tenth to a third. The difference is large enough to have substantial policy implications and to raise some doubts about the meaning of comparisons of productivity figures among countries.

National income statistics are the principle medium through which we see the process of economic growth. We characterize countries as developed or underdeveloped according to their national incomes. Income statistics are also components of measures of the productivity of industries and of the equality of the income distribution. The main point of this book, brought out both by the theory and by the numbers, is that the picture conveyed by national income statistics is often distorted, not because the statistics themselves are inaccurate, nor because they fail to reflect accepted canons of statistical method, but because we attribute to income statistics a social meaning that they do not necessarily possess. Higher income is supposed to mean better off; higher productivity is supposed to mean contributing more to the economic welfare of the community. The theoretical part of the book shows how this association can fail. The empirical part of the book shows that there can be a very great discrepancy between conventional statistics and revised statistics designed to reflect more closely the appropriate social facts. Not only is the discrepancy often large, but it may vary considerably from problem to problem, time to time, or place to place. The consequence of the failure of many income statistics and comparisons among income statistics to bear the desired social implications is that many of our ideas about the nature of economic life in poor countries and about the process of economic growth stand in need of substantial revision.

PART I

THE COMPARISON OF REAL NATIONAL INCOMES IN RICH AND POOR COUNTRIES

1

The Meaning of Real Income

REAL income could be defined statistically. The real income of a country would be the number obtained when certain information is processed in accordance with a set of rules. The statistics cited in the introduction of real national incomes in $U.S. per head could be decreed correct by defining real national income as the outcome of the process by which these statistics were constructed. Equally, these statistics could be decreed incorrect by defining real national income as the outcome of another statistical process yielding a different set of numbers. Or one might have many concepts of real income, each tied to a separate computational rule.

The trouble with this procedure is not merely that statistics might proliferate indefinitely. There is a deeper problem. We use statistics like real income because they tell us something about economic life. They have meanings, or perhaps a family of meanings. Statistics of real income are supposed to demarcate contours of the economic landscape. The concept of real income includes meaning and measurement. It is of the utmost importance that when the meaning is specified, the measurements correspond to that meaning. Statistics must answer the question put to the data and not another question altogether. The defect in the statistics of national income in $U.S. per head in Table 1 is that they do not teach us what we expect to learn from them.

Real income is a concept that arises in income comparisons between countries at a moment of time, between people in one country at different periods of time, and between social classes or trades. Of two men living in the same community, one earning £5000 and the other earning £2500, it may be said that the former is twice as well off as the latter, for whatever the former buys the latter can buy half as much and whatever the latter buys the former can buy twice as much. Frequently we want to make similar comparisons among people or groups of people living in different countries or at different times. The concept of real income is introduced in the hope that we might, for instance, compare the incomes of a typical Thai and a typical Englishman in the same way we compare incomes of two Englishmen in England.

The term 'real income' has been used in economic writing in a variety of ways with a variety of meanings. There are a number of similar, but not identical, questions that might be answered with statistics of real national income. Some of these meanings of real income will now be examined.

In a comparison between Thailand and the U.K.[1] statistics of real income might be constructed to show what multiple of the Thai income, item for item, one could buy in the U.K. at U.K. prices with the average U.K. income. In this comparison the real income of Thailand would be the quantities of items consumed (or invested) in Thailand valued at U.K. prices in £; the corresponding real income of the U.K. would be the U.K. national income in £ exactly as it appears in the official statistics. The ratio of the Thai to the U.K. real national income per head corresponding to this interpretation of real income, is illustrated in Fig. 1. Income consists of only two commodities, grain and machines; amounts of grain and machines consumed per head are measured on the horizontal and vertical axes respectively. Thai and U.K. consumption patterns[2] are shown as points labelled accordingly. Relative prices of grain and machines are indicated on the diagram as slopes. Relative prices in Thailand and the U.K. are the heavy lines drawn through the points representing consumption patterns. In accordance with long-standing economic terminology, these

[1] In the course of this book we shall treat the U.K. and Thailand both as fictional and as real countries. In the diagrams of Parts I and II they are fictional or, at most, representative of any pair of rich and poor countries. It is no more difficult to label countries as U and T than it is to label them in the usual way as A and B, and it is useful to have our diagrams referring to U and T when the analysis is applied to the U.K. and Thailand as real countries in Part III. This convention, and the labelling of commodities as grain and machines rather than by neutral symbols such as Q_1 and Q_2, make the analysis easier to follow, but one must be on one's guard lest propositions about Thailand and the U.K. in Part III be accepted as true merely because they are true of Thailand and the U.K. in Parts I and II.

[2] The word 'income' is often used in the text to refer to national income per head, and income is sometimes spoken of as if it consisted exclusively of

lines are referred to as Thai and U.K. budget constraints. The intersection of the U.K. budget constraint with the vertical axis, the point Y_{UU}, is the national income per head of the U.K. at

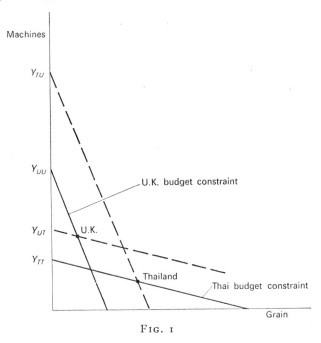

Fig. i

U.K. relative prices valued in units of the machines.[1] Similarly the Thai national income at Thai relative prices valued in machines is Y_{TT}. The dotted lines in the figure are the budget constraints as they would be if U.K. relative prices obtained in Thailand or if Thai relative prices obtained in the U.K. The dotted line through

---

consumption. The principles of income comparison apply equally to consumption goods and to title to consumption goods in the future, represented by ownership of investment goods now.

[1] The national income, $Y_{U\mathscr{L}}$ of the U.K. valued in the ordinary way in £ is
$$Y_{U\mathscr{L}} = P_{GU}Q_{GU} + P_{MU}Q_{MU},$$
where P and Q are price and quantity and the subscripts G, M, U, and T represent grain, machines, the U.K., and Thailand respectively. The U.K. national income expressed in units of machines, and designated as Y_{UU}, is the amount of machines the Englishman could buy with his income if he spent it all on machines. Therefore
$$Y_{UU} = \frac{Y_{U\mathscr{L}}}{P_{MU}} = Q_{MU} + \frac{P_{GU}}{P_{MU}}Q_{GU}.$$

the Thai consumption pattern is parallel to the U.K. budget constraint and the dotted line through the U.K. consumption pattern

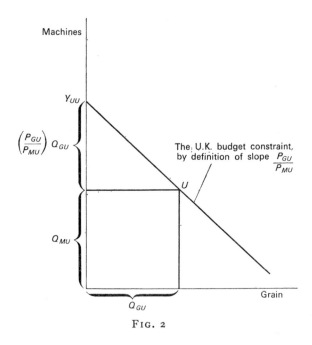

FIG. 2

is parallel to the Thai budget constraint. The points Y_{UT} and Y_{TU} are respectively the U.K. national income valued in machines at Thai relative prices, and the Thai national income valued in machines at U.K. relative prices.[1]

The ratio of Thai and U.K. real incomes that answers the question, 'What multiple of the Thai income per head could

---

We see from this formula and from Fig. 2 that the Y_{UU}, the U.K. income expressed in units of machines, is the intersection of the U.K. budget constraint and the vertical axis, for the distance between Y_{UU} and Q_{MU} is the distance Q_{GU} multiplied by the slope of the budget constraint.

$$[1] \quad Y_{TT} = Q_{MT} + \frac{P_{GT}}{P_{MT}} Q_{GT},$$

$$Y_{UT} = Q_{MU} + \frac{P_{GT}}{P_{MT}} Q_{GU},$$

$$Y_{TU} = Q_{MT} + \frac{P_{GU}}{P_{MU}} Q_{GT}.$$

be bought in the U.K. at U.K. prices with the U.K. income per head?' is Y_{TU}/Y_{UU}, the ratio consumption patterns in the two countries valued in each case at U.K. prices.

There is a reciprocity in income comparisons between people in the same community that does not carry over to comparisons between communities. The Englishman who earns £5000 can buy twice the consumption pattern of the Englishman who earns £2500, and the Englishman who earns £2500 can buy half the consumption pattern of the one who earns £5000. But if the average Englishman can buy twice the consumption pattern of the average Thai, it does not follow that the average Thai can buy half the consumption pattern of the average Englishman; it may be more or less. The reciprocity breaks down because the Englishman and the Thai are confronted with different relative prices. The ratio of the Thai and U.K. real incomes that answers the question, 'What multiple of the U.K. income per head could be brought in Thailand at Thai prices with the Thai income per head?' is Y_{TT}/Y_{UT}, the ratio of consumption patterns in the two countries weighted in each case by Thai relative prices.

The ratios, Y_{TU}/Y_{UU} and Y_{TT}/Y_{UT}, are known as binary comparisons. It is obvious from inspection of Fig. 1 that they need not be equal, for Thailand appears to be the more prosperous of the two countries in the comparison at U.K. prices, and the U.K. appears more prosperous in the comparison at Thai prices. This is to be expected. If tastes in the two countries are similar, people in each country consume relatively more of items that are comparatively cheap, and each country appears relatively, though not absolutely, better off in the comparison at the other country's prices. That these ratios differ does not mean that one is right and the other wrong, or that an average is more appropriate than either. Each ratio answers a separate question. Each ratio has its own meaning within the family of meanings that makes up the concept of real income.

There is another kind of question that statistics of real income might be called upon to answer. An Englishman might want to know not what multiple of the Thai income he could buy but how well off Thai people are by his standards, how large an income it would be necessary to have in the U.K. to be as well off as a typical Thai in Thailand.

To formulate this meaning of real income in a precise way,

suppose that tastes are identical in Thailand and in the U.K. in the sense that a common set of indifference curves applies to both countries. Fig. 3 is the same as Fig. 1 whenever points are labelled identically. The curved lines, U_1 and U_2, are indifference curves applicable both to Thailand and to the U.K. The indifference curve U_1 is the one that happens to contain the Thai consumption

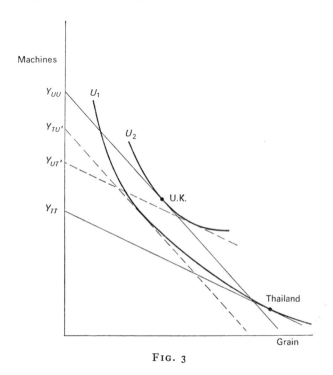

FIG. 3

pattern and the curve U_2 is the one that happens to contain the U.K. consumption pattern, but both curves describe the tastes of both countries. The Thai and U.K. budget constraints are, of course, tangent to U_1 and U_2 respectively, for it is an equilibrium condition, a necessary condition for consumption patterns to be what they are, that market prices reflect the rate of trade-off in use between any two commodities.

Just as there are two binary comparisons, so there are at least two welfare comparisons of real income in Thailand and the U.K. Two distinct welfare questions are:

(a) What proportion of the average U.K. income is necessary to make a man in the U.K. as well off as a typical Thai?

(b) What proportion of the average Thai income is necessary to make a man in Thailand as well off as the typical Englishman?

The ratios of real incomes in Thailand and the U.K. answering these questions are $Y_{TU'}/Y_{UU}$ and $Y_{TT}/Y_{UT'}$, as illustrated in Fig. 3. The value $Y_{TU'}$ is the income (expressed as an amount of machines) that one would need in the U.K. to be as well off as a typical Thai; $Y_{TU'}$ is the smallest income that enables a man confronted with U.K. prices to buy a consumption pattern yielding as much utility as the Thai consumption pattern. The value $Y_{TU'}$ is the intersection with the vertical axis of the tangent to U_1 parallel to the U.K. budget constraint. The value $Y_{UT'}$ is similarly defined.

From now on, the ratios $Y_{TU'}/Y_{UU}$ and $Y_{TT}/Y_{UT'}$ will be spoken of as comparisons 'by U.K. standards' and 'by Thai standards' in contrast to the binary comparisons, Y_{TU}/Y_{UU} and Y_{TT}/Y_{UT}, which are 'at U.K. prices' and 'at Thai prices'. In general, the ratios by Thai and U.K. standards differ from each other and from the binary comparisons. More will be said later about relations among these four ratios.

Identification of real income and welfare rests on three premises which need be only approximately correct. First, it must be possible to summarize tastes of people in a country by community indifference curves. It must be possible to know whether a real or imagined change in income per head makes Englishmen as a whole better off. We would normally say that Englishmen as a whole are better off when there has been an increase in goods and services that could be distributed to make each man better off and when the pattern of income distribution has not changed too much. Second, tastes and community indifference curves should be the same in the countries compared. Of course, consumption patterns in the two countries need not be, and sometimes cannot be, the same. It is consistent with identity of tastes for people of rice-growing countries to eat rice and people in wheat-growing countries to eat wheat as long as each grain is cheaper in the country where it is grown. Identity of tastes means that people in each country would choose the same consumption pattern in the same circumstances, that a typical Thai, living in England and enjoying a typical English income would choose the consumption pattern of a typical Englishman.[1] Third, the welfare interpretation of real income requires that an increase in economic welfare is always the source of an increase in welfare as a whole. Economic welfare is that part of total welfare derived from goods and services, food, clothing, medicine, education, etc. The non-economic components of welfare are the traditions of one's country, the surroundings one is accustomed to, the pleasures of living among one's friends. The use of real income statistics in policy-making requires that there be a correspondence, however rough and approximate, between the numbers claimed to represent economic welfare and human happiness, total welfare, good states of consciousness, or some equivalent psychological or social experience. Were this not so there would be no reason to seek more income rather than less. The enterprise of comparing real national income would be pointless if one did not believe that increases in real income cause increases in welfare as a whole.[2]

[1] It might be possible to dispense with the second premise by specifying which set of community indifference curves is being appealed to in an income comparison. For instance, a comparison might be designed to show how much income an Englishman would need in the U.K. to be as well off as he would be if he had to subsist in Thailand on the average Thai income.

[2] The correspondence between numbers and experience has been examined by Professor S. H. Frankel who describes conditions in which the correspondence may fail to hold. First, income is only part of welfare and what increases income may not increase total welfare if another aspect of welfare is affected adversely in the process. 'Bushmen of South Africa remained hunters because they liked hunting; income to the bushmen was defined in terms of success in the chase and in the sustenance yielded by the chase alone. Such income could not be compared with equivalent goods and services which might have resulted from some other form of activity.' Second, the relation between economic welfare and total welfare may be so constituted that disadvantages in a social system only begin to hurt once a degree of prosperity is obtained. It is just possible that an oppressed minority may become more miserable once prosperity allows it leisure to fully appreciate its situation. Third, the nature and composition of economic welfare is not found outside society, but is formed and determined by the institutions, laws, customs, and beliefs of a society. Total welfare gives meaning to economic welfare and not the other way around. In contrast to our usual model of economic life based on cold, rational, selfish, economic man, Professor Frankel poses the analogy of economic activity as a game with income as the score, 'To identify, or seek for, a functional relationship between income and total welfare is as logically fallacious as to identify points scored in playing a game with the "value" of the game to the players' ('Psychic and Accounting Concepts of Income and Welfare', *Oxford Economic Papers*, 1952 and reprinted as Essay III of Professor Frankel's book *The Economic Impact on Underdeveloped Societies*).

Closely allied to the welfare interpretation of real income is the notion of productivity in comparisons of the contribution to the economy of the different trades or sectors. In this context productivity is measured as income per man employed. Productivity statistics might be designed to answer questions such as 'Is there an appropriate allocation of labour among industries?' or 'Would the nation as a whole be made better off by the transfer of labour from one industry to another, for instance, from agriculture to manufacturing?'

Statistics of real income may be constructed for special purposes, like measuring a country's capacity to make or participate in war or its ability to share in the cost of international organizations. The U.N. statistics cited in the introduction were constructed with the latter object in mind. Those statistics are probably more satisfactory indicators of the burden of taxes than of economic welfare. The military interpretation of real income approaches the fringe of the concept. It is questionable whether flows of commodities weighted by prices chosen to reveal the fighting capacity of a nation ought to be considered as income at all. Price weights used for this purpose would differ considerably from weights designed to reveal comparative welfare.

Finally, statistics of real income, however interpreted, are used as pegs on which to hang other characteristics of the economy. For instance, one might ask whether there is a greater degree of equality in the distribution of income in poor countries than in rich countries, whether or to what extent economic progress increases the proportion of the labour force in manufacturing, whether rich countries grow faster than poor countries, whether consumption as a proportion of income or consumption of some variety of goods increases as a country becomes better off, whether social mobility, literacy, or political freedom can be associated in any way with prosperity, whether velocity of money is an increasing function of real national income, and so on. Answer to questions of this kind require at a minimum that a correlation be shown between statistics of real national income among countries or over time and some other social or economic fact.

Real income comparisons may be over space or over time. In this book we are concerned with comparisons over space, with real income comparisons among countries, with productivity comparisons among industries, and with measures of equality or inequality of income. We are not concerned, except incidentally, with measures of economic growth.

The statistician preparing measurements of real national income has as his guide the desired meaning of real income; he tailors his calculations to the specifications set by the question or questions to be answered by the statistics.[1] Though many of the meanings of real national income give rise to the same kinds of measurement problems, and though even a clear statement of the meaning of real income does not resolve all of the statistical and computational issues on which the statistician must exercise his judgement, it is best in discussing measurement problems to have in mind a single meaning of real income, a particular question that the statistics are designed to answer. In what follows real income is to be a measure of economic welfare. Think of a comparison of real income between Thailand and the U.K., designed to answer the question 'How much money would one need in England to be as well off as a typical Thai?' Real income is compared in the two countries by revaluing quantities in both countries at a common set of prices. Revaluation of income requires three kinds of decisions by the statistician. He must determine the scope of income, what is included in income, and what is not; he must divide the total flow of income into quantities of a single set of commodities; and he must choose a set of prices at which quantities may be valued. These decisions will now be examined, one by one.

[1] It is of course open to the statistician to say that he is undertaking such and such a calculation which the user may interpret as he pleases, but then it is open to the user to adjust the calculation to his own purposes and neither the original statistic nor the revision has any particular right to the title of the measure of real income.

2

The Scope of Income

AT the fringe of the concept of income are items about which there are differences of opinion as to whether they belong in income or not. This chapter is a brief examination of the fringe in an attempt to determine how a widening or a narrowing of the scope of income might affect income comparison between rich and poor countries. Two general considerations might be emphasized before we get down to details.

First, in a comparison of income between two countries, the definitions of income, in the countries must be economically congruent, and not merely the same. Imagine a comparison of real income between an industrial country that imports all its food and a peasant economy based on subsistence farming. A definition of income that limited the scope of income to commodities actually traded in the market might be technically the same for both countries. The statistician compiling the national incomes would apply the same rules and procedures to both countries. Nevertheless, the definitions of income in the two countries would be incongruent from an economic point of view because food is included in the definition of income in one country and excluded from the definition of income in the other.

Second, the choice of items to be included in income requires a balancing of subjective and objective considerations. Requirements of the concept of real income conflict with the need for reasonably accurate statistics that do not depend too much on the individual judgement of the statistician. Housewives' services is a case in point. Income as a flow of goods and services should include the services of housewives, but as there is no market setting a price for housewives' services, as we cannot say whether their value should increase or decrease over time, and as there are many housewives, the decision to include housewives' services in income would cause the estimate of the rate of growth of real income to depend in large measure on the statistician's choice of how housewives' services are to be valued. Housewives' services are excluded from income because we want a comparison of incomes to be reasonably independent of the judgement of the statistician and not because we believe that housewives' services should not be there. How far one dares go with introducing questionable items into comparisons of income depends in part on who one happens to be. The independent scholar has much more freedom in this matter than does the government statistician who quite properly must justify his figures by generally accepted statistical criteria.

There is a standard rule in the national income accounting that the national income includes all goods and services produced during the year, exclusive of intermediate products, with deduction for depreciation. Each of the three key phrases in this rule, 'goods and services', 'intermediate products', and 'depreciation', gives rise to a number of problems and the examination of the scope of income can be subdivided under these headings.

(a) GOODS AND SERVICES

In most countries the scope of national income is not limited to commodities bought and sold. The usual practice is for some commodities not exchanged for money, because they are consumed by the producer or because they are bartered, to be included in income at imputed values. Among the imputations in the British national income are rents of owner-occupied houses and of publicly-owned buildings, farm produce consumed by the farmer, and employees' remuneration in kind, like free coal for miners and food and lodging for the armed forces. Most of the national incomes of the underdeveloped countries automatically include imputations for subsistence agriculture[1] because value added in agriculture is computed from estimates of total production. Recreation, funerals, religious services, domestic services, and indigenous medicine provided outside the market sector in a peasant economy are sometimes included in a national income and sometimes not. These items ought to be fully included in a comparison with a country where they are part of income because they are within the market sector.

[1] In *The Income of Nations* (p. 177), Paul Studenski notes that the farmers' consumption of home-grown food as a percentage of total farm income was 26 per cent in Ireland in 1953 and 18 per cent in Canada in 1950. I estimate that the comparable figure for Thailand now is over 50 per cent.

Though it is generally recognized that goods and services produced in the non-market sector of an economy ought to be included in income at imputed prices, the obvious extension of this argument to processes is usually overlooked. When wheat grown and consumed on the farm is included in income, it is as a rule valued at the farm-gate price, at the price the farmer would receive for the wheat if he sold it. But wheat must be milled into flour and the flour must be baked before the wheat may be consumed as bread. To value home consumption of wheat at farm-gate prices is, implicitly, to exclude home milling and home baking. The case for including home milling and baking in income is exactly analogous to the case for including home-grown food. If two countries are alike except that bread is baked commercially in one country and at home in the other, we would want a comparison of real incomes to show these countries to be equally well off, for people in both countries receive the same flow of goods and services. A comparison of incomes would show the country where bread is baked commercially to have the larger real income unless flour consumed in the other country were valued at the price of bread. As economic development takes place, goods enter the home in a more finished form. People buy bread instead of flour, ready-made clothing instead of cloth, furniture instead of wood. Incomes of poor countries tend to be biased down in income comparisons unless processes as well as goods are included in income at imputed prices.[1]

[1] I think that the rate of economic growth of countries is often over-estimated because values are not imputed for economic processes undertaken in the home. Consider as an example the consumption of cereal products in the United States between 1889 and 1919. Though the evidence is somewhat shaky for the years before 1909, it appears that cereal consumption in the United States has been declining since at least 1889. Consumption of wheat flour and corn meal together fell from 342 pounds per head in 1889 to 227 pounds in 1919. (The estimate for 1889 is from M. K. Bennett *The World's Food* Harper Brothers, 1954, and the estimate for 1919 is from *Historical Statistics of the United States.*)

The national accounts present a different picture. The most reliable estimate of the U.S. national income at the beginning of this century is that of the National Bureau of Economic Research. The estimate of the real value of cereal consumption in the National Bureau's accounts for that period is that of W. H. Shaw (*Value of Commodity Output Since 1869* National Bureau of Economic Research, 1947). The results of his calculation are shown in the first five rows of table 2. The percentages are calculated as follows: Values of total consumption in 1889 and 1919 are divided by the product of the population and the price level. The ratios of the resulting numbers are then expressed as percentage increases over

A case can be made for including housewives' services as part of income. There is a well-known example in economics of the man who increases national income by divorcing his wife and hiring her as a housekeeper; the housekeeper's wage is part of income while the same service performed by a wife is not. Estimates of the value of housewives' services have occasionally been

---

the value for the earlier year. In calculating his series of values in constant dollars, Shaw used one price index for all food products.

Comparing the top and the bottom rows of table 2, we see that though cereal consumption per head fell by a third, the estimate in the accounts of the real value per head of cereal consumption rose by a quarter. Part of the discrepancy is probably attributable to the price index. Part may be due to the exclusion of minor grains in the bottom row. But part is surely due to the increase in commercial baking over the period. The share of bread and bakery products in the total value of cereals consumed rose from about a quarter in 1889 ($128 million out of a total of $519 million) and to almost a half in 1919 ($1,151 million out of $2,519 million).

Had the national accounts shown a 24% decline in the real value of cereal consumption instead of 33% rise, the estimate of the growth of G.N.P. per head between 1889 and 1919 would be reduced from 79·7% to 77·1%.

TABLE 2

Estimates of Percentage Increases in Consumption per Head of Cereal Products in the United States between 1889 and 1919

Value in constant dollars of all cereal products consumed	24·3%
The above includes (a) 'Bread and bakery products'	130·1%
(b) 'Hominy and grits, oatmeal, breakfast food, and all other cereal products'	111·7%
(c) Flour: wheat, corn, rye, buckwheat, barley	—11·8%
(d) Wheat, corn, rye, buckwheat consumed in farm households.	—2·8%
Apparent civilian consumption of corn flour and meal, and of wheat flour	—33·5%

Source: The fifth row is from M. K. Bennett *The World's Food* p. 166 and *Historical Statistics of the United States* series 581 and 582. Values of income in current dollars are from W. H. Shaw *Value of Commodity Output Since 1869*. Items (a), (b) and (c) are from pp. 108–10. Item (d) is from pp. 247–8. The price index is 1 on p. 290.

included in the national income accounts, raising income from 10 to 25 per cent. As has already been mentioned, the reason for not including housewives' services in income is that the value of this item cannot be accurately measured.[1]

If housewives' services are excluded from income, then substitutes for housewive's services might be excluded also. Laundries, bakeries, washing machines, and vacuum cleaners perform services in the market sector that would otherwise be performed in the household sector. Either the inclusion in income of housewives' services or the exclusion of substitutes for housewives' services would increase incomes of poor countries relative to incomes of rich countries. It is true that commercial firms producing substitutes for housewives' services or mechanical aids to housewives may contribute to the welfare of the community by allowing the housewife more leisure, but this is insufficient justification for the inclusion of this item in an income comparison. First and most important, it is inappropriate to include marginal increments to leisure in an income comparison when leisure as a whole is excluded. This argument has particular force in a comparison between an industrial society and a peasant society. One would not want to include a labour-saving expense as part of the income of an industrial society, if leisure as a whole is excluded, for the balance of leisure may, for all we know, favour the peasant society.[2]

Second, the net effect of labour-saving devices may not be an increase in leisure. It may instead be to allow more women to enter the labour force. If this is the result, the effect of labour-saving devices is counted twice in the national accounts, once directly when the labour-saving devices are sold and a second time in the value of the goods and services produced by the woman who can enter the labour force because she is relieved of household chores.

The services of public capital, roads, hospitals, and public buildings might also be included in real income. These items are excluded because of the difficulty of measuring their contribution. The net effect of this exclusion is as a rule to bias down the

---

[1] See Studenski, op. cit. p. 177.

[2] Leisure as a whole is excluded from income because of difficulties in measuring its contribution. In principle, if two countries are enjoying this same flow of goods and services we would like to say that one has the higher income if it can get the goods and services at less expenditure of leisure time.

incomes of rich countries especially, because rich countries typically have relatively large stocks of public goods.

(b) INTERMEDIATE PRODUCTS

A more interesting set of problems arises in the interpretation of the rule for distinguishing between final products and intermediate products. The reason for distinguishing between final and intermediate products is to avoid double counting, to ensure that each item produced is included once and only once in the accounts, and not repeatedly as it is sold from firm to firm on the way to the final consumer. Since it is not possible to examine every commodity to determine whether it contributes to economic welfare directly or as a component of another commodity, intermediate products are identified by their purchasers. Purchases by firms of items that are normally kept for less than a year are counted as costs of production or intermediate products, and these purchases are not recorded in the national accounts. All purchases by consumers and by government, and purchases of investment goods by firms are recorded as final products in the national accounts. This rule identifies most of the items we would like to consider as final products, but it falls short of our requirements in two opposite ways; it classifies work expenses borne by the householder as final product, and it excludes expenses by the employer for the convenience, training, and safety of the employee.

Expenditure on transport to work is frequently classified as income when it ought to be cost of production. Transport to work confers no net benefit on the worker; it is a cost incurred in the process of procuring goods and services already recorded in the national accounts. The rule for distinguishing final products from intermediate products, or from cost of production, records transport to work as part of income when the worker pays for it, and as an intermediate product when the employer pays for it. An employer who arranges and pays for the transport of his workers from their homes to their place of work can increase the national income by charging them for the service and raising their wages accordingly.

Anomalies like this do not matter much when income statistics are used to measure economic growth in a single country. The advantages of having an unambiguous rule for the statistician to follow far outweighs the disadvantage in this misclassification of expenditures. But the rule can be quite misleading in comparisons of real incomes between countries with vastly different social and economic characteristics. Transport to work in one's own car or by purchased transport, the accompanying inflation of site rents in cities, and expenses in aleviating congestion of cities and air polution are all wholly or partly costs of production misclassified as income. The importance from our point of view of these costs of production of industrial societies is that they have no counterparts in primitive communities. Only in industrial societies do men need to travel ten or fifteen miles a day from home to work. Consequently, failure of the conventional rule to classify these items correctly tends to create a systematic bias in the income figures, making industrial societies appear richer than they really are.

On the other hand, part of the expenditure of a rich country on transport to work represents a convenience to workers made possible by the fact that they are relatively well off. Whether or not transport to work should be counted as a final product in a comparison between a rich country and a poor country depends on the nature of the alternative. If the alternative to riding to work is walking to work and the average distance between home and the place of work is about the same in both societies, then transport to work is a net benefit to industrial society. But if the peasant lives near his land and the separation between home and place of work is a characteristic unique to industrial society, then transport to work is a cost of production borne, like all costs of production, to reap benefits that are already recorded in the accounts.

Public services are in a sense intermediate and a case can be made for their exclusion from income. By public services we mean, of course, not all the activities of government, not railroads or public industry or the post office, but only those that do not yield marketable goods and services. The services that might be excluded from income are the cost of Parliament, of the Ministry of Finance, of the Home Office, etc. Their exclusion is not because they are unproductive but because they create the social conditions necessary to the functioning of the economy and their benefits accrue in the total output of goods and services already recorded in the national accounts. Public services are like the steel that goes into an automobile; both are necessary for production but neither enters directly into income.[1]

Instances cited so far of the failure of the conventional rule to distinguish accurately between final and intermediate products have been associated with expenditure by final consumers or government that are really costs of production, and the effect of the bias has been to make rich countries appear richer than they are. The other class of deviation from the rule tends to have the opposite effect. Expenditures by firms for the benefit and safety of employees are more important in rich, industrial societies than in poor, peasant societies. Incomes in rich societies are understated if working conditions are better in rich societies than in poor, and if this difference in working conditions involves firms in expenses not recorded in the accounts. On-the-job training, which should appear in income under the heading of education, is missing because the worker does not pay the employer for the experience. This item may even be deducted from income, for the worker may accept a lower wage than his services could command elsewhere.[2]

Closely related to the distinction between final products and intermediate products is the question of what to do with expenditures in one country on services that are provided free by nature in another. Heating costs is the important instance. There is no doubt that expenditures on heating, or air conditioning, belong in income in a welfare comparison in a single country between different periods of time, for a comfortable temperature is unquestionably a component of welfare. But consider an income

---

[1] An Hungarian income estimate prepared in the 1930s excluded government services on the grounds that governments do not 'produce values in addition to the flow of consumer goods, but ensure only the maintenance of the present economic and social order . . . and the present level of production'. A similar view has been expressed by S. Kuznets and the force of the argument has been recognized by J. R. Hicks. However, Professor Hicks argued that in practice one should not try to separate out intermediate products of government because 'we want to measure something and not to arrive at a figure for the national income which is what it is because we say it is'. The discussion is reviewed in Studenski, op. cit., Chapter 14; sources of the quotations may be found there.

[2] S. Kuznets increased the pre-war national income of China from $37 to $65·5 per head by the following corrections. (1) He magnified the part of the Chinese income associated with raw materials by the ratio of raw materials to finished products in the United States because only raw materials were included in the Chinese income, while finished products appeared in the American income, and because, one way or another, the Chinese raw materials had to be processed and distributed in order to be consumed. (2) He increased the

comparison between a country with an ideal climate where no heating cost is required, and a country where heating cost, in the form of direct expenditure on fuel, warm clothing, and well-insulated housing, comprises a large proportion of income.[1] If prices were the same in both countries, a man would prefer to live in the country with the ideal climate unless his income in the cold country were sufficiently larger than his income in the other country to compensate for heating cost. Consequently an income comparison designed to compare economic welfare between these countries might exclude heating cost from the income of the cold country because it is a cost of production of conditions provided free by nature in the warmer country.

But one environment is rarely better than another in every respect. An environment that does not require heating may require air conditioning or special precautions against earthquakes. It is difficult to decide where the balance lies; environmental defects may cancel out, or they may favour one place or another, as in a comparison between Alaska and California. The issue is complicated by the fact that air conditioning is a luxury and heating is a necessity. The poor in Scotland spend a larger proportion of their incomes on heating than do the poor in South-East Asia and there is no doubt that life without heating in Scotland is far more difficult than life without air-conditioning in South-East Asia. Yet the very rich in South-East Asia may spend as much on air-conditioning as the very rich in Scotland spend on heating. Expenditure on heating and air conditioning may or may not be excluded from income in a comparison between Scotland

---

Chinese income by the proportion of services to total income in the United States; services on this calculation comprised (a) items outside the market in China but inside the market in the United States, domestic services, funerals, religion, furniture, etc., (b) banking services, (c) urban rents and transport to work, (d) government. Professor Kuznets estimated the proportion of each of the above items that represented a net benefit to the United States in comparison with China, and he used only the residual in scaling up the Chinese income. See 'National Income and Industrial Structure, *Econometrica*, Supplement, July 1949'. The original Chinese estimate in dollars was that of Mr. Ta Chung Liu (*China's National Income, 1931–1936*, Brookings Institution, 1946).

[1] I have estimated that the total cost of keeping warm in the U.K., including heating, extra clothing, and well-insulated buildings, comes to about £60 per head per annum out of a total income of £406. See 'The Thai National Income at United Kingdom Prices,' *Bulletin of the Oxford University Institute of Statistics*, 1963.

and South East Asia, depending on whether it is the condition of the rich or the poor that is emphasized.

(c) CONVENTIONS ABOUT DEPRECIATION

Income is defined as the amount of goods and services the economy might consume during the year consistent with being as well off at the end of the year as at the beginning. Income is divided into consumption and investment; investment is measured net of depreciation, for we should not wish to say that a country is well off merely because it produces a large amount of capital goods to restore its depreciating stock. This principle might be extended in two ways both of which are relevant to income comparisons between rich and poor countries.

First, an allowance might be made in the accounts for human depreciation associated with the gradual ageing of the labour force. Most educational expenditure is required to maintain the general level of education and only a small proportion can be said to make the standard of education higher at the end of the year than it was at the beginning. Virtually all primary and secondary education and part of university education in the rich industrial countries is a cost of maintenance of the stock of human capital and only improvements in the standard or extent of education can be accounted as net final product.

Second, the phrase 'as well off at the end of the year as at the beginning' might be interpreted per head instead of in total. The conventional measure of depreciation might be revised to define net investment as the excess of investment above that necessary, not merely to maintain the total capital, but to preserve the proportion between the capital stock and the population. This revised convention would reveal whether or not a country is preparing to increase income per head. For instance, if gross national product is 100, investment is 30, depreciation is 5 per cent of capital, population growth is 3 per cent, and the capital stock is 500, then the net national income and net investment computed in the usual way are 75 and 5 respectively. But a 3 per cent rate of population growth requires an increase in the capital stock of 15 to preserve the capital–labour ratio and keep people as well off at the end of the year as they were at the beginning. On this basis, national income is only 60 and net investment is −10.

There are statistical obstacles in the way of this calculation because we often do not know the capital stock and because in practice the growth of income in the long run is due more to technical change than to pure investment. But income statistics prepared under present conventions may show positive net investment when a country is, in fact, becoming less and less well-prepared economically as time goes on. An alternative income comparison among countries in which investment is measured net of the cost of maintaining capital per head might show which among them are really preparing to be better off in the future.

3

Commodities

HAVING decided upon the scope of income, what is to be included and what is not, the statistician is confronted with the task of converting the total flow of income into amounts of a finite number of commodities. This is a most important aspect of income comparison and one that is almost invariably overlooked in discussions of the subject.

Difficulties in choosing commodities are best illustrated in an example. Suppose a statistician is estimating real income in Thailand and the U.K. He wants to compare economic welfare, and he

TABLE 3

A Detailed Specification of Commodities

Commodities	Thailand Quantity consumed (kilo)	Price (baht)	United Kingdom Quantity consumed (kilo)	Price (£)
mangoes	200	1	1	3
apples	1	10	200	0·2
buffalo meat	100	5	1	15
beef	1	50	100	0·8
rice flour	1000	1	1	3
wheat flour	1	10	1000	0·1

believes that the best indicator of economic welfare is an average of the binary comparisons. He calculates two ratios of real incomes, one at Thai prices and the other at U.K. prices, and his final comparison is their geometric average.[1] Prices and quantities are shown in Table 3.

The Thai consume relatively large amounts of tropical products —mangoes, buffalo meat, and rice flour—which are inexpensive in Thailand—and relatively small amounts of the temperate products—apples, beef, and wheat flour—which are expensive because they have to be imported or because it is difficult to produce them locally. Similarly people in the United Kingdom consume large amounts of temperate products and small amounts of tropical products. Obviously the binary comparisons are far apart because the income of the U.K. appears enormous at Thai prices and the income of Thailand appears enormous at U.K. prices.

Let $Y_{U£}$, $Y_{U\,baht}$, $Y_{T£}$, $Y_{T\,baht}$ be the incomes of the United Kingdom and of Thailand, expressed in pounds and baht respectively. Multiplying the appropriate prices and quantities, we see that

$$Y_{U£} = £241 \qquad Y_{T£} = £5201\cdot1,$$
$$Y_{U\,baht} = 17\,007 \text{ baht} \qquad Y_{T\,baht} = 1770 \text{ baht},$$

and that the ratios of the Thai and U.K. incomes valued in pounds and baht respectively are

$$\frac{Y_{T£}}{Y_{U£}} = \frac{5101\cdot1}{240} = 21\cdot1,$$

$$\frac{Y_{T\,baht}}{Y_{U\,baht}} = \frac{17\,007}{1770} = 0\cdot104.$$

In this example the income of Thailand is either twenty times that of the U.K. or only one tenth, depending on price weights.

Real income might have been compared in a different way. Suppose that instead of accepting the commodities in detail as the basic units of the comparison, the statistician had decided to use only fruit, meat, and flour as commodity units and to price them at unit values in each country. Table 3 is now reduced to the form shown in Table 4.

---

[1] This average is called Fisher's ideal index number.

A glance at Table 4 reveals that this revised calculation makes the real incomes of the two countries equal because their consumption patterns are identical. The average of the binary comparisons from Table 3 gives a different result; the geometric average of 21·1 and 0·104 is 1·46; the real income of Thailand

TABLE 4

A Broad Specification of Commodities

Commodities[1]	Thailand		U.K.	
	Quantity consumed (kilo)	Price (baht)	Quantity consumed (kilo)	Price (£)
fruit	201	1·04	201	0·21
meat	101	5·45	101	0·94
flour	1001	1·01	1001	0·10

appears to be about half as much again as that of the U.K. We have concocted this example to make the comparison in terms of a few, in a sense artificial, commodities appear right, while the binary comparisons based on a detailed enumeration of commodities, and the geometric average of the binary comparisons appear wrong on almost any interpretation of income as a welfare measure. Another example could have yielded a different result. The choice of common commodities is rarely as easy as in our example.

As much as he dislikes imposing his judgements onto the data, the statistician cannot avoid having to choose a common set of commodities for, in principle and possibly even in practice, there is no limit to the extent of subdivision of commodities. We started the example as if all mangoes, apples, beef, etc., were homogeneous. This in itself implies a judgement about the compara-

---

[1] The prices are calculated by dividing the total value of the items included in the table by the total quantity. Take fruit in Thailand as an example. The total value is 210 baht, 200 kilos of mangoes at 1 baht per kilo plus 1 kilo of apples at 10 baht per kilo. The unit value of a kilo of fruit is 1·04 baht (210/201) per kilo.

bility of grades of meat, and of sizes and varieties of mangoes or apples, etc. As a rule the appropriate detail in specification of commodities depends on the degree of similarity between the countries. A comparison of income between United States and European countries can withstand a fine breakdown of incomes without creating an excessive dispersion between the results of the binary comparisons. An attempt to compare the income of a European country with that of an agricultural country in the tropics could yield results like those in our example if the number of commodities were too large.[1]

[1] S. Kuznets has expressed the hope that the choice of commodities could ultimately be made on scientific principles. 'The eventual solution would obviously lie in deriving a single yardstick that would be applied to both types of economies—a yardstick that would perhaps be outside the different economic and social institutions and would be grounded in experimental science (of nutrition, warmth, health, shelter, etc.)'. ('National Income and Industrial Structure'. *Econometrica* 1949, Supplement, p. 225.)

4

Prices

THE choice of prices in an income comparison between Thailand and the U.K. would present no difficulty if a welfare comparison by Thai standards required that quantities in both incomes be valued at Thai prices, and a welfare comparison by U.K. standards required that quantities in both incomes be valued at U.K. prices. As our chosen example is of a comparison by U.K. standards designed to answer the question, 'What proportion of the U.K. income per head, is required in the U.K. to make a man as well off as an average Thai?', the U.K. prices would be appropriate.

There are circumstances in which comparison by U.K. standards requires U.K. price weights. Suppose that the difference between the Thai and U.K. consumption patterns were attributable entirely to the fact that the people of Thailand, who are relatively poor, consume necessities—food, simple clothing, simple housing —while the people of England consume relatively more luxuries—cars, T.V. sets, and quality products of all kinds. An Englishman with the real income of the average Thai would acquire the Thai consumption pattern because he too would have to reserve his income for the necessities of life. In this case the standard of living of the Thai could be unambiguously assessed as the value of the Thai consumption pattern at U.K. prices, and the simple identification of our welfare question with U.K. price weights is correct. Similarly the question, 'What proportion of the Thai income per head is needed in Thailand to make one as well off as an average man in the U.K.?', could be answered by an income comparison at Thai prices.

Identification of the welfare questions with price weights must be qualified in an important respect. Differences in consumption patterns may be influenced by relative prices as well as by real income. The value of the Thai consumption pattern at U.K. prices is greater than the real income of Thailand assessed by U.K. standards because an Englishman in England with enough money to buy the typical Thai consumption pattern, can make himself better off than he would be with the average Thai income in Thailand by changing the consumption pattern, buying less of goods that are relatively expensive in the U.K. and more of the goods that are relatively cheap.

If relative prices alone determined consumption patterns, the two welfare questions would point to the same ratio of real incomes somewhere between the binary comparisons. If real income alone determined consumption patterns, the two welfare questions would be answered by the two binary comparisons. Usually, the truth lies between these extremes; the answers to the two welfare questions are distinct ratios of real income, but these ratios are not identical to the binary comparisons, and almost always lie between them.

AN EXAMPLE OF THE CHOICE OF PRICES

The relation between welfare questions and the choice of price weights is illustrated in Fig. 4, which is, in effect, Fig. 3 superimposed on Fig. 1. Again there are two commodities, grain and machines, consumed in different proportions by people in Thailand and the U.K. Relative prices of grain and machines are assumed to be different in the two countries, for otherwise there could be no doubt about the appropriate choice of price weights. Tastes are identical in the two countries, in the sense that people in both countries share a common set of indifference curves. Income per head in the U.K., indicated by the point U, consists of 2 units of grain and 4 units of machines. Income per head in Thailand, indicated by the point T, consists of 2 units of grain and 1 unit of machines. Two indifference curves are illustrated, one passing through the point U and the other passing through the point T. As in Fig. 1, the unbroken lines tangent to indifference curves at U and T are budget constraints. The slopes of the budget constraints, indicating prices of grain in terms of machines, are 2 in the U.K. and $\frac{1}{2}$ in Thailand, and their intersections with the vertical axis are:

Y_{UU}, the income per head of the U.K. valued at U.K. relative prices in amounts of machines, and

Y_{TT}, the income per head of Thailand valued at Thai relative prices in amounts of machines.

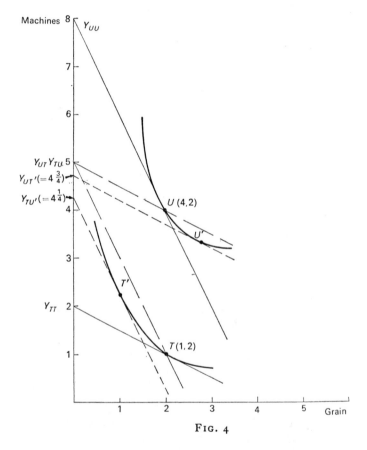

FIG. 4

Also as in Fig. 1, the broken lines through U and T are each parallel to the budget constraint of the other country, and their intersections with the vertical axis are:

Y_{UT}, the income per head of the U.K. valued at Thai relative prices in amounts of machines, and

Y_{TU}, the income per head of Thailand valued at U.K. relative prices in amounts of machines.

Values of these incomes are:

$$Y_{TT} = 2, \qquad Y_{TU} = 5,$$
$$Y_{UT} = 5, \qquad Y_{UU} = 8;$$

and the binary comparisons, the ratios of U.K. to Thai income at Thai and U.K. prices respectively, are:

at Thai prices $\qquad Y_{UT}/Y_{TT} = 2\cdot5,$

and at U.K. prices $\qquad Y_{UU}/Y_{TU} = 1\cdot6.$

However, neither binary comparison is in itself a sufficient index of comparative welfare. An Englishman with enough income in Thailand to duplicate his old consumption pattern may take advantage of the change in relative price to make himself better off than he was by buying more grain and less machines; for in Thailand grain is relatively cheap and machines are relatively dear. The income in Thailand that makes an Englishman as well off as he was at home is not his old consumption pattern valued at Thai prices, but an income just sufficient to keep him on his old indifference curve. This income, indicated as in Fig. 3 by the point $Y_{UT'}$ on the diagram, is valued at $4\frac{3}{4}$ units of machines. Similarly, a Thai is as well off in the U.K. as he was at home if he has an income, indicated by the point $Y_{TU'}$, of $4\frac{1}{4}$ units of machines.

The answers to the two questions about comparative welfare are therefore provided, not by the binary comparisons, but by the ratios

$$\frac{Y_{UU}}{Y_{TU'}} = 8 \div 4\frac{3}{4} = 1\cdot67$$

and

$$\frac{Y_{UT'}}{Y_{TT}} = 4\frac{1}{4} \div 2 = 2\cdot13.$$

In this example the average Thai is as well off as an Englishman who has to subsist on three-fifths of the average income in the U.K., and the average Englishman is as well off as a Thai who earns 213 per cent of the average Thai income.

Of the four ratios, $\dfrac{Y_{UU}}{Y_{TU}}, \dfrac{Y_{UT}}{Y_{TT}}, \dfrac{Y_{UU}}{Y_{TU'}}$, and $\dfrac{Y_{UT'}}{Y_{TT}}$, the first pair, the binary comparisons, may be computed directly from statistics of prices and quantities in Thailand and the U.K., but does not provide the answers to our welfare questions; and the second pair provides the answers we require but cannot in practice be computed from statistics of prices and quantities because we do not normally know the extent of substitution that would take place if a resident of one country were confronted with prices in another.

This opens the general question of how closely the ratios of real income assessed by the standards of Thailand and the U.K. can be estimated from the binary comparisons. In our example, the binary comparisons bracket the other two ratios and the four ratios stand in the relation

$$\frac{Y_{UU}}{Y_{TU}} \leqslant \frac{Y_{UU}}{Y_{TU'}} \leqslant \frac{Y_{UT'}}{Y_{TT}} \leqslant \frac{Y_{UT}}{Y_{TT}}.$$
$$(1 \cdot 60) \quad (1 \cdot 67) \quad (1 \cdot 88) \quad (2 \cdot 50)$$

Is this relation a universal characteristic of income comparisons or an accidental consequence of the numbers chosen in our example? This question is of some importance because, if the relation is universal, it provides justification for using an average of the binary comparison as an index of economic welfare.

The first and third of these inequalities always hold because $Y_{TU'}$ is necessarily less than Y_{TU}, and $Y_{UT'}$ is necessarily less than Y_{UT}; this may be seen at a glance from Fig. 4. In addition, the income of the U.K. appears greater at Thai prices than at U.K. prices ($Y_{UU}/Y_{TU} < Y_{UT}/Y_{TT}$) whenever people in each country consume relatively more of the goods that are relatively cheap. One can construct queer cases in which people do not consume more of goods that are relatively cheap, but these cases may be ignored for all practical purposes.

The middle inequality does not always hold, but cases in which it does hold are of considerable practical importance. The truth or falsehood of the relation

$$\frac{Y_{UU}}{Y_{TU'}} \leqslant \frac{Y_{UT'}}{Y_{TT}},$$

indicating that the income of each country appears small when the comparison is by its own standards, depends on why the countries consume different proportions of grain and machines. As tastes are assumed to be the same, there are only two possible explanations, and they are not mutually exclusive: the Thai consume relatively more grain because grain is cheaper in Thailand or because grain is an inferior good and the Thai are relatively poor. If the difference in the proportions of grain and machines consumed is due entirely to the difference in relative prices,[1] then the ratios $Y_{UU}/Y_{TU'}$ and $Y_{UT'}/Y_{TT}$ are equal. If, on the other hand, the difference in consumption patterns is largely due to differences in real income, if the Thai would continue to consume relatively more grain than do the English even if prices were the same in both countries, then $Y_{UU}/Y_{TU'}$ is always strictly less than $Y_{UT'}/Y_{TT}$. The point U' tends to lie quite close to U, and the point T' tends to be quite close to T; $\dfrac{Y_{UU}}{Y_{TU'}}$ is only slightly greater than $\dfrac{Y_{UU}}{Y_{TU}}$, and $\dfrac{Y_{UT'}}{Y_{TT}}$ is only slightly less than $\dfrac{Y_{UT}}{Y_{TT}}$; and the relation $\dfrac{Y_{UU}}{Y_{TU}} \leqslant \dfrac{Y_{UT}}{Y_{TT}}$, ensures that $\dfrac{Y_{UU}}{Y_{TU}} \leqslant \dfrac{Y_{UT'}}{Y_{TT}}$ be true as well. It is only when price effects and income effects push in opposite directions that the second of the three inequalities may fail to hold.

In short, the binary comparisons flank the two welfare comparisons, and each of the welfare comparisons lies closer to its corresponding binary comparison whenever differences in income reinforce the effects of differences in relative prices on consumption patterns. There is reason to believe that this is generally the case in comparisons between rich and poor countries. The necessities of life—food, poor housing, low quality clothing—are usually cheap in poor countries, while the luxuries—cars, radios, fine houses, high quality clothing and consumer durables—are relatively dear.

The bracketing of the true welfare comparisons by the binary comparisons is the justification for the common practice of using an average of the binary comparisons as a single welfare measure. The commonly used statistic is the geometric average, Fisher's ideal index number, which in our example turns out to be

$$\sqrt{\left(\frac{Y_{UU}}{Y_{TU}} \times \frac{Y_{UT}}{Y_{TT}} \right)} = 2.$$

Let us now return to the question posed at the outset of the examination of the choice of prices. Suppose we want a measure

---

[1] In this case all indifference curves have the same shape, and one indifference curve is a scaled-down model of another.

representing $\dfrac{Y_{UU}}{Y_{TU'}}$ the ratio of the real incomes of Thailand and

the U.K. assessed by the standards of the U.K. We know that the

$\dfrac{Y_{UU}}{Y_{TU}}$ is an underestimate. We also know that the Fisher's index lies

within the range between $\dfrac{Y_{UU}}{Y_{TU}}$ and $\dfrac{Y_{UT}}{Y_{TT}}$. The choice between

$\dfrac{Y_{UU}}{Y_{TU}}$ and the Fisher index depends on our guess about the size of

the error. We prefer to use $\dfrac{Y_{UU}}{Y_{TU}}$ if we believe that the substitution

effect is small in comparison with the distance between the binary comparisons. Otherwise the Fisher index is preferred. Our example turns out to make the comparison at U.K. prices (1·60) come out closer to the comparison of real income by U.K. standards (1·67) than does the comparison based on the geometric average of the binary comparisons (2·00). This is of course a consequence of the numbers we have chosen and a different choice of numbers could have given a different result. The example, used in examining the choice of commodities and summarized in Table 3, is one in which the substitution effect predominates over the income effect so that a geometric average of the binary comparisons is a much better indicator of economic welfare than either binary comparison taken by itself.

There is a close connection between the choice of items to be subsumed under a single commodity in an income comparison and the problem of balancing-off substitution effects and income effects in the choice of price weights. Items are treated as units of the same commodity if they are close substitutes, in the special sense that the consumption of each good would be sensitive to changes in the price of the other if both goods were plentiful.[1] In choosing commodities, one first amalgamates the very close substitutes, like big apples and little apples, into a single commodity. If fewer commodities are desired, the most substitutable of the commodities, like apples and mangoes, are themselves amalgamated into broader commodities which are then treated as if they were homogeneous stuff. A fine breakdown of the flow of

---

[1] Many definitions of substitutes are possible. One might employ a chemical or physiological definition. Apples and mangoes might be considered as sub-

income into commodities—mangoes, apples, rice, flour, etc.—
leaves considerable room for substitution among them; the binary
comparisons go very far apart and an average of the two is usually
preferred to either as a measure of economic welfare. In a broader,
less-detailed specification of commodities, one in which wheat
flour and rice flour are considered as one commodity, and apples
and mangoes are considered as another, the main possibilities for
substituting among items in income are eliminated. The binary
comparisons come closer together, income effects account for a
larger part of the remaining spread between the binary comparisons, and the case for using U.K. prices to represent U.K.
standards becomes stronger.

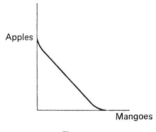

FIG. 5

When the object of an income comparison is to show how much
it would cost in the U.K. to buy a bundle of goods that would
make an Englishman as well off as a typical resident of an underdeveloped country, the best estimate of real income might be one
at U.K. prices with commodities broadly specified to lessen the
influence on the comparison of prices of rare luxuries like mangoes
in the U.K. or brussels sprouts in Thailand. The fact that the

---

stitutes if they contained similar proportions of calories, vitamins, etc. The
definition employed here is economic. Two commodities are substitutes if the
quantity demanded of each is significantly influenced by the price of the other
when both commodities are plentiful. The last phrase is essential for without it
mangoes and apples would not be substitutes at all. The presumed relation
between apples and mangoes is illustrated in Fig. 5. An indifference curve of
apples and mangoes is a straight line except in the regions near the axes. There
is some critical relative price of apples and mangoes such that if apples are
cheaper, fruit consumption consists almost entirely of apples, and if mangoes are
cheaper, fruit consists almost entirely of mangoes. The curved portions of the
indifference curves reflect rare and special uses of apples and mangoes that
persist even when the relative price changes.

British income looks enormous to the resident of the under-developed country because cars, radios, T.V. sets, etc., are very expensive (and very rare) in the underdeveloped country is irrelevant to the purpose of the comparison. A statistician from an underdeveloped country who wants to know how well off the English are by his standards would value commodities differently. An international organization trying to satisfy both parties might take an average of the comparisons computed from the two points of view.

5

Some Attempts to Measure Real National Income

REAL income cannot be measured exactly. The difficulty is not the usual one, common to all measurements, of calibration. It is not just that our scales are inaccurate, though they are to some extent. It is that we do not know what scales to apply. There is no substitute for the judgement of the statistician in deciding what scope of income, what division into commodities, and which prices are most suited to his purpose. With this reservation in mind we shall survey some attempts to measure real income and shall observe the numbers arrived at in these studies. Broadly speaking, studies of real income are of two kinds: attempts to compare incomes at a common set of prices, and short-cuts of which the U.N. statistics, cited above, are an example. Since no method carries unimpeachable credentials, all bear scrutiny, and most yield information of value.

(a) REVALUING INCOMES AT A SINGLE SET OF PRICES

Many attempts have been made to compare real income among countries by valuing quantities at one or more common sets of prices. Perhaps the best known example is the work of Colin Clark in *The Conditions of Economic Progress* (1940). As price weights, he employed what he called 'oriental units' representing the purchasing power of a rupee in India, and 'international units' representing the purchasing power of a U.S. dollar.

Comparisons of the real incomes of the United States and several European countries at American and 'average European' prices, were prepared by M. Gilbert and I. Kravis under the auspices of the O.E.C.D.[1] Some results of this study, together with comparisons between the United States and China and between the United States and the Soviet Union, are presented in Table 5. The statistics are not entirely comparable, because they have been compiled at different times, by different people, and for different

TABLE 5

Real National Incomes Per Head Expressed as Percentages of the Real National Income Per Head of the United States

	(1) Ratios of incomes in local currencies weighted by the foreign exchange rate between the local currency and $U.S.	(2) Ratios of incomes at U.S. prices	(3) Ratios of incomes at local prices	(4) Geometric average of (2) and (3)
U.K. (1955)	42	64	51	57
France (1955)	47	56	43	49
Italy (1955)	19	35	24	29
U.S.S.R. (1955)	—	45	22	31
China (1952)	2·5	6·1	1·8	3·3

Sources: The estimates for the U.K., France, and Italy are from M. Gilbert and Associates *Comparative National Products and Price Levels*, Table 4, p. 28. The estimates for the U.S.S.R. are from *Comparisons of United States and Soviet Economies*, Joint Economic Committee, Congress of the United States, 1959. The estimates for China are from W. W. Hollister *China's Gross National Product and Social Accounts 1950–1957*.

[1] Previously the International Labour Office had performed similar computations in measuring costs of living in different countries. See H. Staehle, *International Comparisons of Food Costs*, I.L.O., 1934. This work includes references to older literature on the subject.

purposes; they are placed together in the table to illustrate orders of magnitude. Without exception the real incomes of all the countries, except of course the United States, appear larger at American price weights than at local price weights. Of special importance for this study is the fact that countries appear better off in comparison with the United States when incomes are measured at a common set of price weights than when they are converted into $U.S. by the foreign exchange rate. This fact is in contradiction to the purchasing power parity doctrine and to what one would expect from economic theory. Explanation of this fact is one of the main themes of Part II.

The comparison between China and the United States in Table 5 is only one of many attempts to compare national income of developed and underdeveloped countries. M. F. Millikan has estimated that the real income of many African and Asian countries is 350 per cent larger than indicated by the usual statistics of $U.S. per head, and E. E. Hagen has estimated that the comparable figure for Burma is over 300 per cent.[1]

(b) THE SOCIAL ADEQUACY METHOD

A rough measure of welfare cutting out many of the problems we have examined can be obtained by expressing incomes as multiples of the subsistence level. In each country income per head in the local currency is divided by an estimate of the cost of subsistence; the quotient of income per head and the cost of subsistence is the measure of real income. In a comparison of income between Japan and the United States, this method[2] raised the ratio of the Japanese to the American income almost 600 per cent over what it appears to be when incomes in local currencies are converted to a common currency through the foreign exchange rate.

This method has defects. First, as there is no firm line of division between subsistence and non-subsistence other than the purely physiological one (which is not the definition employed, for we

[1] Both estimates are cited in C. Kindelberger, *Economic Development*, Chapter 1.

[2] A. H. Gleason, 'The Social Adequacy Method of International Level of Living Comparisons as Applied to Japan and the United States', *The Journal of Economic Behaviour*, April 1961.

often speak of people *living* on less than a subsistence income), the result of the comparison depends in a fundamental way on judgements about what constitutes subsistence. Governments compute estimates of income necessary for a 'minimum' standard of living. There is no assurance that definitions are standardized from one country to another. It often turns out that people in rich countries suppose the minimum subsistence income to be relatively high, while people in poor countries suppose the minimum subsistence income to be relatively low. Second, among countries that are well above subsistence, it may happen that one has an income which is the larger multiple of the subsistence level, while another is actually better off because prices of goods bought in addition to what is needed to subsist are relatively low.

(c) COMPARISONS EMPHASIZING A FEW COMMODITIES

Attempts have been made to simplify international comparison of economic welfare by emphasizing one or more key indicators, chosen because they represent an important component of welfare or because they are thought to be correlated with income as a whole. The simplest and in some respects most useful indicator of this type is 'grain equivalents'; national income (or some part of it—consumption, wages, or agricultural output) may be compared among countries in grain equivalents by dividing money values by grain prices.[1] The representation of income in kilos of grain instead of money has a good deal in common with the social adequacy method of income comparison because the minimum subsistence income is often closely related to grain price. Though this measure suffers from many of the same defects as the social adequacy method, it can be used with some effect to show the standard of living of the poor[2]

Standards of living in different countries may be expressed as weighted averages of several quantities of goods and services produced or consumed.[3] The difficulty with this type of

[1] In the example illustrated in Fig. 1, the Thai and U.K. incomes, Y_{TT} and Y_{UU}, are expressed in machine equivalents.

[2] See 'Agricultural Progress Measured in Grain Equivalents', Chapter IV of C. Clark and M. R. Haswell, *The Economics of Subsistence Agriculture* (1964).

[3] See M. K. Bennett, 'International Disparities in Consumption Levels', *American Economic Review*, Sept. 1951.

comparison is knowing how to weight indices in the final comparison. A weighting that emphasizes agricultural production or food consumption tends to overstate the incomes of the poorer countries, while a weighting that emphasizes industrial products, radios, cars, and the like, tends to overstate the incomes of the richer countries.

(d) PROJECTIONS

If suitable estimates of real income are available for some countries, and a correlation can be established between these estimates and statistics about other social facts, the correlation may be used to predict or project real incomes of countries for which direct estimates are not available. The method of projections was first used to correct U.N. statistics of national income in U.S. dollars per head estimated through the foreign exchange rate, in the light of direct comparisons of incomes at common prices. The U.N. figures are available for many countries; direct comparisons are available for only a few. It was found that, among countries where both types of national income comparison were available, the orderings of countries on the scale of rich and poor were about the same in the two methods of comparison, but the absolute values differed considerably; the ratio of highest to lowest income was far larger in the U.N. comparison than in the direct comparison. This relationship may be observed among the statistics in Table 5 above. The direct comparison was believed to be right, and a correction factor was applied to the U.N. comparison. Incomes were raised by different proportions depending on their place on the scale; lowest incomes were raised most, medium incomes were raised less, and the highest incomes were not raised at all. The correction factors were chosen to make the spread between high and low incomes about the same in the direct comparison at a common set of prices and in the U.N. comparison altered in this way. This rule for correcting the U.N. figures was applied to the incomes of all countries. Using this technique J. P. Delahut and E. S. Kirschen[1] concluded that national incomes per head of countries with incomes of less than $50 U.S. as estimated by the U.N. ought on the average to be increased by

[1] 'Les revenus nationaux de monde non cumministe', *Cahiers Economiques de Bruxelles* No. 10, April 1961.

211 per cent. The technique has been extended by W. Beckerman[1] who based income projections on economic indicators like tons of steel consumed and numbers of letters dispatched rather than on the U.N. figures.

Projections may be labour-saving and they may reveal useful facts about recurrent patterns of economic behaviour, but they do not in any respect solve or circumvent the conceptual problems discussed above. First, the projections are never perfect. Invariably a relation between real income and other variables is subject to a margin of error. We cannot know how close a projection is to the true figure until the true figure has been calculated. Second, the projections computed so far do not lend themselves to the break-down of real income by sectors like industries, final uses, or earnings of social classes. Third, and most important, a projection requires something to project from. Initially there must be a set of real incomes which we choose to call 'correct', and from which we estimate relations for projecting other incomes. All of the conceptual problems discussed above enter into the projections in the way the initial 'correct' incomes are chosen. If the manner of measuring the 'correct' incomes of, for instance, under-developed countries in the tropics is such as to make these incomes appear high, then high incomes will be projected on to other under-developed countries in the tropics. This sort of problem might be partially overcome by restricting the initial 'correct' incomes to industrial countries with similar social and economic structures, but only at the cost of having to assume without evidence that relations observed among these countries apply to other countries elsewhere. Ultimately a projection is not an independent system of income measurement on a par with those we have been discussing. It is instead a mixture of hypotheses about similarities among economies, and a way of guessing some incomes from others.

(e) COMPARISON THROUGH THE FOREIGN EXCHANGE RATE

This is the method used by the United Nations in constructing the statistics cited in Table 1. The economics of this method of income comparison is examined in detail in Part II.

[1] *International Comparisons of Real Incomes*, O.E.C.D., 1966.

PART II

WHY PRICES VARY FROM PLACE TO PLACE AND HOW GEOGRAPHICAL PRICE VARIATION AFFECTS INCOME COMPARISONS

6

Introduction: The Purchasing Power Parity Doctrine and its Implications

IN Part II we discuss matters which may at first seem to have little to do with one another but which are in fact closely related. First, we extend the range of the study to cover all types of income comparison including comparison among regions of a country, measurement of equality or inequality of the income distribution among persons or social classes, comparison of savings ratios and expenditure patterns among countries, and comparison of income per man employed in different industries as measures of productivity. Productivity is singled out for attention because it is of interest in itself and because difficulties in interpreting productivity statistics are typical of the difficulties encountered in many types of income comparison. Second, we study the geography of prices. So far, geographical price spreads of identical commodities have been accepted as unexplained facts. From now on we shall be concerned with the forces that cause prices of identical commodities to differ from place to place. Knowledge of how statistics came to be what they are, assists us in interpreting their meaning and in correcting the statistics if they fail to signify what we would like them to. Third, we try to explain the discrepancy between the results, summarized in Table 5, of income comparison through the foreign exchange rate and income comparison by valuing quantities at a set of prices common to all countries compared.

The connection between these issues may be seen by focusing on the third—the failure of the U.N. statistics cited in Table 1 to measure what we expect them to. Though these statistics are wide of the mark, the method by which they were constructed has a good deal to recommend it. The justification of the method is closely associated with the purchasing power parity doctrine which we shall now examine briefly.

The purchasing power parity doctrine is that 'the rate of exchange between the home currency and the foreign currency must tend in equilibrium to be the ratio between the purchasing powers of the home currency at home and the foreign currency in the foreign country. This ratio between the respective home purchasing powers of the two currencies is designated "purchasing power parity".'[1] This shall be our working definition, but to make it precise, we must specify what is meant by 'the ratio between the purchasing powers of the home currency at home and the foreign currency in the foreign country'. The ratio of purchasing powers depends on what one proposes to buy. The ratio is different for each commodity and for each bundle of goods. Two promising candidates for 'the' ratio between purchasing powers are (a) the ratio of the costs of the bundle of goods consumed in the home country and (b) the ratio of the costs of the bundle of goods consumed in the foreign country. It suits our purpose to define the purchasing power parity doctrine rather broadly as valid whenever the foreign exchange rate lies between these ratios. Specifically, in a comparison between Thailand and the U.K., the purchasing power parity doctrine states that

either $\qquad P_U \leqslant F \leqslant P_T \qquad$ (1a)

or $\qquad P_T \leqslant F \leqslant P_U,$ (1b)

depending on which of the two expressions, P_U, and P_T, is the larger, where F is the foreign exchange rate between the baht and the £ (baht per £),

$\quad P_U$ is the ratio of purchasing powers of the baht and the £ with respect to the bundle of goods consumed in the U.K., and

$\quad P_T$ is the ratio of purchasing powers of the baht and the £ with respect to the bundle of goods consumed in Thailand.

The expressions P_U and P_T are

$$P_U = \frac{\sum_i P_{iT} Q_{iU}}{\sum_i P_{iU} Q_{iU}} \quad \text{and} \quad P_T = \frac{\sum_i P_{iT} Q_{iT}}{\sum_i P_{iU} Q_{iT}},$$

[1] J. M. Keynes, *A Tract on Monetary Reform*, Macmillan and Co., 1923, p. 88.

where the i designate commodities, P_{iT} is the Thai price of the i commodity, etc., and statistics of quantity are per head rather than in total.

The formula chosen to represent the purchasing power parity doctrine is mathematically equivalent to the statement that a comparison of incomes through the foreign exchange rate lies between the binary comparisons. Multiply all the elements of formula 1 by the factor $Y_{U\,\pounds}/Y_{T\,baht}$, where $Y_{U\,\pounds}$ is the money national income of the U.K., equal to

$$\sum_i P_{iU}Q_{iU}$$

and $Y_{T\,baht}$ is the money national income of Thailand, equal to

$$\sum_i P_{iT}Q_{iT}.$$

Some of the terms cancel, and equation (1) is transformed into either

$$\frac{\sum_i P_{iT}Q_{iU}}{\sum_i P_{iT}Q_{iT}} \leqslant \frac{Y_{U\pounds}F}{Y_{T\,baht}} \leqslant \frac{\sum_i P_{iU}Q_{iU}}{\sum_i P_{iU}Q_{iT}} \qquad (2a)$$

or

$$\frac{\sum_i P_{iU}Q_{iU}}{\sum_i P_{iU}Q_{iT}} \leqslant \frac{Y_{U\pounds}F}{Y_{T\,baht}} \leqslant \frac{\sum_i P_{iT}Q_{iU}}{\sum_i P_{iT}Q_{iT}} \qquad (2b)$$

Equation (2b) is by far the most likely of the two cases because each income in a comparison seems relatively large at the other country's prices. The first and third terms are the binary comparisons at U.K. and Thai prices respectively. The middle term is the ratio of national incomes in local currencies adjusted by the foreign exchange rate: it is precisely the formula used in constructing the statistics of national income per head in Table 1 in the introduction.

Consider once again the income comparisons summarized in Table 5 of Part 1. The statement of the purchasing power parity doctrine in formula 2 carries the clear implication that the values in column 1 should be between the values in columns 2 and 3. This is true of only two countries in the table. For all other countries, real income appears smaller when valued through the foreign exchange rate than in either binary comparison.

Reasons for the failure of the purchasing power parity doctrine will be discussed in later chapters. As a background to that discussion, we shall in this chapter consider reasons why the doctrine is often thought to be true. One important reason is that arbitrage forces prices to conform to a purchasing power parity: In the absence of transport costs or other impediments to international movements of goods and services, the prices of each good in the U.K. must equal its price in Thailand multiplied by the foreign exchange rate between baht and £, for were this not so for any particular good, a man could make a profit buying the good in one country and selling it in the other. If cloth sells at five baht a yard in Thailand and one shilling a yard in England, if the exchange is fifty-eight baht to the pound, and if cloth can be moved costlessly from England to Thailand, then a trader can make any amount of profit by buying cloth in England and selling it in Thailand. Were this configuration of cloth prices and the foreign exchange rate to arise, the attempt of traders to profit by arbitrage would either raise the cloth price in England or lower it in Thailand or alter the exchange rate until the purchasing power parity in cloth is restored. The argument applies to each good separately and to income as a whole, and it implies that relative prices are the same in both countries and that absolute prices in the local currencies differ by a factor equal to the foreign exchange rate. Absolute prices become the same everywhere when all prices are converted by the foreign exchange rate from the local currencies to a common currency such as $U.S. When there are transport and distribution costs, relative prices and prices expressed in $U.S. differ from country to country according to the direction of international trade; exports of each country are relatively cheap there and imports are relatively dear. The purchasing power parity doctrine is based on the expectation that the highs and lows cancel out, leaving the over-all cost of living about the same in any two countries when all prices are expressed in the international currency.

Plausible as this expectation may be, it turns out to be wrong. The highs and lows of prices do not cancel out. Instead prices are systematically high in some countries and systematically low in other countries. It seems that prices in underdeveloped countries tend to be systematically low, and prices in developed countries or rich countries seem to be systematically high.

One implication of the arbitrage argument is beyond dispute. It makes no difference to the results of an income comparison whether countries use a single currency in common or have separate local currencies as long as the separate currencies are freely convertible at a foreign exchange rate. Suppose Scotland became an independent country, linked to England by a customs union without tariff barriers or restrictions on trade of any kind. Scotland establishes a new currency unit but does not alter its economy in any other way. In these circumstances the national income of Scotland, computed in Scottish £ and converted to U.K. £ by the foreign exchange rate between Scottish £ and U.K. £, would be just equal to the old income in U.K. £ of Scotland before the change in its political status. By assumption none of the quantities in income have changed. The prospect of arbitrage assures that each price in Scottish £ equals the old price in U.K. £ multiplied by the foreign exchange rate, for were this not so traders could profit by altering the direction of trade. Consequently, it is possible to speak about a world price structure even when each country has its own currency. Prices in all currencies may be converted into gold, dollars, or any other currency by the foreign exchange rates. It makes no difference which currency is chosen as the world currency, for the structure of relative prices throughout the world and the ratios of incomes of countries are the same whichever currency is chosen. Henceforth when we speak without special reference of income comparisons in money terms, it is to be understood that we mean either a comparison between two places or sectors using the same currency or, what amounts to the same thing, a comparison of incomes converted to a common currency by foreign exchange rates.

The two interpretations of the phrase 'in money terms' are equivalent when currencies are freely convertible. The equivalence breaks down in a world of multiple exchange rates or direct restrictions on currency movements. Throughout Part II we make an assumption even stronger than convertibility. It is assumed that exchange rates are in equilibrium in the sense that they are consistent with a balance of trade everywhere. This could come about through a system of fluctuating exchange rates, or through a gold standard, or through a system of fixed exchange rates if rates were pegged appropriately. In reality some exchange rates are not in equilibrium, and there are formidable theoretical and practical obstacles in the way of finding out how much an actual exchange rate differs from the equilibrium rate in a free market. We have chosen to ignore this problem because our inquiry is limited to the assessment of income comparison in circumstances where the market works well. If the market is not allowed to work well, if official exchange rates differ from those required to clear the market of goods and money, a new free market exchange rate must be estimated before the analysis we are concerned with can begin.[1]

When goods can be moved costlessly from place to place, the foreign exchange rate equals the purchasing power parity for each good individually and for income as a whole. Consequently, divergence between foreign exchange rate and the purchasing power parity must be sought in the mechanism that keeps prices apart. The components of price gaps between locations are easily enumerated. They are listed in Fig. 6 for a comparison between Thailand and the U.K. Income in each country is divided into traded and untraded goods, defined here as products that enter into international trade and products that do not. A differential between Thailand and the U.K. in prices of identical products entering into international trade may be divided into five parts, internal transport and distribution cost in Thailand, tariffs or export taxes in Thailand, international transport cost, tariffs or export taxes in the U.K., and internal transport and distribution cost in the U.K. In each country the total condition of production and consumption sets the rate of trade-off between goods that enter into international trade and goods that do not. The relative price of untraded goods in Thailand and the U.K. is in a sense the product of the rates of trade-off between untraded and traded goods in Thailand, between traded goods in Thailand and traded goods in the U.K. and between traded and untraded goods in the U.K.

When currencies are convertible and trade is balanced, income comparisons in money terms are independent, not only of currency units, but even of frontiers between states. It made no difference

[1] Since official exchange rates may have been pegged too high or too low, the United Nations has prepared statistics of national income in $U.S. per head based on estimates of equilibrium exchange rates. See *Yearbook of National Accounts Statistics* 1964, Part D, Table 6b. This revision of the statistics does not on the whole make the underdeveloped countries appear better off. In principle there are only two possible ways in which the foreign exchange rate could fail to reflect purchasing power parity. Either exchange rates are not in equilibrium in the sense that they are not consistent with a balance of payments, or the world price structure allows prices to be generally lower in some areas than in others. The available evidence, which is admittedly fragmentary, suggests that disequilibrium exchange rates are not the major determinant of the anomalous pattern in Table 5, and that the main explanation of this pattern is to be found in the operation of the international price mechanism.

to the comparison between Scotland and England whether these regions were separate states or part of one state. If a comparison of money incomes among countries may yield a biased comparison of real incomes, so too may a comparison of money incomes among regions. The same forces act in the same way in both situations. This point is frequently overlooked. Though it is well-recognized that income comparisons among countries through

Fig. 6

The Chain of Prices between Thailand and the U.K.

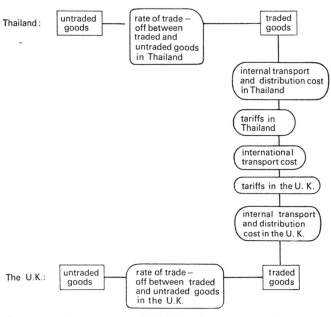

the foreign exchange rate yield biased estimates of real income as a measure of economic welfare, money income is usually accepted without question as an index of economic welfare among regions. This practice may be inappropriate, for price levels may differ among regions. Similarly, if industries are located in different places, it may be inappropriate to use income per man employed by industry as a measure of productivity because equal incomes earned at different places may represent different amounts of goods and different contributions to economic welfare.

Arbitrage is not the only support of the purchasing power parity doctrine, for the doctrine is implied by the principle of income maximization in economic theory. In economic theory it is assumed that all factors of production are deployed to maximize money income: labourers maximize wages, firms maximize profits, landlords maximize rents, and so on. The justification for this criterion of economic behaviour on the supply side of the economy is that income is a surrogate for utility. No matter what his taste, a man is better off with more money than with less. Similarly a man who creates a larger income is more productive than a man who creates a smaller income. Hence income per man employed is the correct measure of productivity and income per head by regions is the correct indicator of prosperity. As stated in the textbooks, the principle has no geographical limits. It is true in a city, in a region, in a nation, and in the world. On this inter- pretation of the principle of income maximization, employment earning $40 U.S. is preferred to employment earning $39 U.S., not only when both are available in the United States, but even when one employment is available in the United States and the other is available in Ethiopia. If men maximize money income, seek the highest wage or the greatest profit, then dollars must yield the same satisfaction everywhere and the purchasing power parity doctrine must be valid no matter what the statistical evidence to the contrary. To maintain that the purchasing power parity doctrine is false, we must modify or abandon the principle of income maximization. This issue is the subject of the next chapter.

To sum up, four main arguments support the view that the statistics cited in Table 1 of the introduction, statistics of national income in $U.S. per head computed by dividing money income by the product of the population and the foreign exchange rate are adequate indicators of real income. First, of all the measures we have examined, they are the easiest to compute and the least subject to influence by the judgement of the statistician. Second, the purchasing power parity doctrine implies that a ratio of incomes in money terms ought to lie within the range of the binary com- parisons. Third, since statistics of money income are acceptable in measures of the equality or inequality of the income distribution in a country, in measures of productivity, and as measures of real income of regions within a country, they ought, as shown in the Scottish–English example, to be acceptable in comparison among countries. Finally there is the argument from economic theory.

Firms are operated and resources are deployed to maximize money income; this behaviour is only rational if money income is a reflection of real income; therefore money income must be a reflection of real income.

The four arguments have different status. The first is undeniably true but it is no justification for treating money income as representative of real income unless the representation is known to be reasonably accurate. The second is not logically binding. The purchasing power parity doctrine rests on the premise that, since trade between two countries is normally in both directions, highs and lows of prices should balance off leaving price levels in the two countries about the same. This is no more than a tendency, a potential which, as will be shown in later chapters, is not fully realized. The third argument is valid but its import is not that the procedure for comparing incomes within a country justifies international comparison in money terms. Rather, the absurdities that arise when national incomes are compared in money terms cast suspicion on procedures for comparing incomes among regions or trades within a country. The fourth argument is also correct in that it follows from its premises. If income maximization is a valid principle without qualification as to geography, then the statistics in Table I must be right. Since these statistics are manifestly inaccurate, the principle of income maximization must be qualified. It is important to determine the geographical limits of the principle of income maximization not only to clear up this ambiguity in economic theory but also to evaluate income comparison among social classes, trades, and regions in a country.

From now on we shall frequently refer to this or that method of income comparison as being biased. The concept of bias in income comparison must be sharpened and carefully defined, if it is to serve us in the demonstration of how each of the forces causing prices to differ from place to place affects income comparison. Real income, the object of the comparison, will from now on be treated exclusively as a measure of economic welfare, with reference to a set of indifference curves supposed to represent the tastes of all parties concerned. Three tests of bias are employed: First, bias may be assessed directly from the indifference curves. A rule for measuring real income is biased if it attributes different real incomes to identical consumption patterns or to consumption patterns lying on the same indifference curve. This is the strongest possible test. Where applicable, it reveals bias no matter how small, but it does not distinguish a large bias from a small one.

Second, bias may be assessed with reference to the binary comparisons, because, as demonstrated in Part I, the binary comparisons tend to span ratios of real income representing economic welfare. A method of income comparison is a biased indicator of comparative economic welfare if it generates ratios of incomes outside the binary comparisons. This is a weak test; there is little merit in passing the test but much suspicion cast on a technique of comparison that fails to do so. Knowledge that a method of income comparison always yields ratios between the binary comparisons is not in itself assurance that the method is a good one, but to know that a ratio is outside the binary comparisons is to be reasonably sure that the means of comparison is defective in some way. This second test is the most useful of the three for our purpose. We wish to show that a method of income comparison between countries or sectors, may fail significantly to perform as is expected of it. A test that shows up large biases is exactly what is required, for when a measure is shown to fail, it matters little that it might have been less than perfect even if it had passed.[1]

A third test of bias used in the discussion of tariffs where neither of the other two can be applied is simply to show that a variable which has no connection with welfare has a strong independent effect on the results of an income comparison.

---

[1] The sensitivity of this test depends significantly on how commodities are defined. Recall the mango, apple example of Part I. The range between the binary comparisons is very wide in a detailed specification of commodities, but becomes successively narrower as the number of commodities is reduced. The likelihood of the ratio of money incomes lying between the binary comparisons is greater when the range between them is wide that when it is narrow, i.e. when the flow of income is broken up into many goods instead of just a few.

7

Real Income and Money Income

THE proposition in textbooks of economics that producers maximize money income is not qualified by geography. Absence of geographical qualification may mean one of two things: It may mean, and is often taken to mean, that geography is as irrelevant to the principle of income maximization as colour and odour are to Newton's laws. On this interpretation, the principle of income maximization is valid over all geographies—cities, provinces, countries, continents, or regions of any size—just as Newton's laws are valid for matter of all colours. Alternatively a geographical qualification may be implicit in one or more of the assumptions of economics. In view of the statistics in Tables 1 and 5, the latter interpretation must be the correct one. Our problem in this chapter is to reveal the geographical assumptions in economic theory and to specify the geographical limits of the principle of income maximization.

A variety of assumptions are possible. Passing from the less to the more restrictive, it might be said that the principle of income maximization is valid across international frontiers when exchange rates are in equilibrium in the sense that they are consistent with a balance of payments, or that it is valid across international frontiers when there are no tariffs or restrictions on currency movements, or that it is valid within countries but not among countries, or that it is only valid in a region small enough for prices of identical products to be the same everywhere. In the course of this chapter we shall argue that, with one important reservation, this last and most restrictive qualification is the correct one, the other qualifications being necessary but insufficient and incomplete. As a producer and as consumer, that is, on the supply side and on the demand side of the economy, economic man maximizes utility. It is usually assumed that as a producer, economic man maximizes utility by maximizing money income. This assumption is true only of an economy condensed into a point or of an economy within which prices are invariant from place to place to place. With a few important exceptions, economic theory is expounded with reference to a market in which this condition is met. Though expositions of economic theory do not as a rule refer to geography, they invariably contain an assumption which sharply limits the kinds of geography that are possible. This assumption is that every commodity has one, and only one, price. The assumption is a reasonable one for most problems that economists are called upon to deal with. For practical purposes in applications of the theory of demand and of the theory of the firm, geographical variation of prices is not large enough to affect the analysis to any significant extent. The assumption that each commodity has one price is so innocuous in most contexts that it is frequently overlooked and not recognized as an assumption at all. Nevertheless the assumption is there and it is only true of a market at a point. We are confronted with a problem in which the assumption is far from innocuous, in which prices vary considerably from place to place, and in which geographical variation in prices is a large part of what we are trying to understand.

That money income is not necessarily an indicator of welfare within a region in which prices differ from place to place, may be seen from a simple example. Suppose a man has to choose between living and working in the city where wages and prices are high, and living and working on a farm where prices and wages are low. High wages in the city are not in themselves sufficient to induce him to work there; a rational man (*homo economicus*) compares the ratios of wages and the cost of living in the city and in the country, and chooses the location where the ratio is highest. In short he maximizes real income rather than money income.

Suppose that real income in the country turns out to be larger than real income in the city even though money income is larger in the city. A statistician asked to prepare estimates of income per head in the country and in the city would produce a set of statistics showing income in the city to be greater than income in the country. Obviously this would not indicate that city people are better off.

Similarly a statistician asked to prepare estimates of rural and urban productivities would if he followed the usual rules, measure productivity in each sector by the ratio of total income in the sector to the corresponding labour force. Assuming that the income shares accruing to factors of production other than labour are the same in both sectors, differences in productivities in the sectors follow differences in wages. The productivity figures show that urban workers are more productive than rural workers, even though rural workers are better off. Whether we should call these statistics biased depends on what we had expected to learn from them. One implication that we would normally expect of productivity statistics is that if productivity is higher in one sector than in another, and if the shares of the non-human factors of production are the same in both sectors, then a movement of labour from the sector where productivity is low to the sector where productivity is high should increase the total product and create the possibility of making everyone better off than he was before. This implication does not follow in our example because the sector with the higher measured productivity has the lower real wage.

This sort of problem cannot arise within the usual framework of economic analysis because of the implicit assumption of a market at a point, as is easily illustrated in a two-commodity world.

Both halves of Fig. 7 show the indifference curves of a man in a market with two commodities, grain and machines. Incomes are expressed in amounts of machines, just as in the derivation of a demand curve. The first half of the figure (a) illustrates assumptions in the usual model of economic analysis. As there are only two commodities, there can be only one relative price, and this price is the same throughout the whole market. Consequently budget constraints corresponding to different wage rates are parallel. Clearly a man who can choose among the wages W_1, W_2, and W_3 picks the highest because this puts him on to the highest indifference curve. The second half of the figure (b) illustrates choices facing a man who is deciding where to live and work within a country where prices as well as wages differ from place to place. Now the highest wage does not necessarily place him on the best possible utility curve, because this wage might correspond to an especially unfavourable price ratio betwen grain and machines. In Fig. 7(b) the best of the options shown corresponds to a wage W_2 which is not the highest that could be obtained.

(a) A GEOGRAPHICAL MODEL OF THE LABOUR MARKET

Our departure from the usual one-point world of economic analysis has so far led us to the two-point world of the city-country example and to the three point world of Fig. 7(b). Some

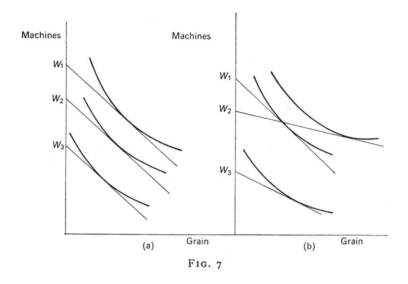

FIG. 7

interesting applications of geographical price variation emerge when the analysis is extended to a continuous geography, the simplest type being a line.

Imagine a country with a territory consisting of a line of length D^*; any location in the country can be referred to by a number D in the range (O, D^*). The advantage of a line over an area is that location on a line can be indicated by a single number rather than by a pair of numbers like latitude and longitude.

We shall first examine the choice of location of a labourer in response to a given configuration of prices and wages at all possible locations. Then we shall derive a relation between prices and wages in different places consistent with equilibrium in the labour market. Suppose that prices and wage rates at each location D are indicated by a set of functions $P_1(D) \ldots P_n(D)$ and $W(D)$, where the subscripts 1 to n refer to commodities. A labourer with a utility function $U(Q_1 \ldots Q_n)$ is free to choose a location D. At that location he would be paid the going wage $W(D)$ and he would have to pay the going prices $P_1(D) \ldots P_n(D)$ for the goods $Q_1 \ldots Q_n$ that he consumes. He would purchase a bundle of goods $Q_1(D) \ldots Q_n(D)$ chosen to make the marginal utility of each good proportional to its price

$$U_i\{(Q_1(D) \ldots Q_n(D)\} = \mu(D)P_i(D)$$
$$i = 1 \ldots n \tag{1}$$

subject to the constraint that the value of expenditure equals the wage.

$$W(D) = \sum_i Q_i(D)P_i(D). \tag{2}$$

Equations (1) and (2) together determine a set of functions indicating the patterns of consumption at all possible locations.

Characteristics of the optimum location are revealed by a few simple manipulations of equations (1) and (2). The total derivative of the wage with respect to location is

$$\frac{dW(D)}{dD} = \sum_i P_i(D)\frac{dQ_i(D)}{dD} + \sum_i Q_i(D)\frac{dP_i(D)}{dD} \tag{3}$$

and the total derivative of utility with respect to location is

$$\frac{dU}{dD} = \sum_i U_i \frac{dQ_i(D)}{dD}. \tag{4}$$

Substituting for U_i in equation (4) by its value in equation (1) yields

$$\frac{dU}{dD} = \mu(D)\sum_i P_i(D)\frac{dQ_i(D)}{dD}, \tag{5}$$

and substituting for $\sum_i P_i(D)\frac{dQ_i(D)}{dD}$ in equation (3) by its value in equation (5) yields

$$\frac{dW(D)}{dD} = \frac{1}{\mu(D)}\frac{dU}{dD} + \sum_i Q_i(D)\frac{dP_i(D)}{dD}, \tag{6}$$

which has a simple economic interpretation: The term $\sum_i Q_i(D)$ $\frac{dP_i(D)}{dD}$ is a quantity weighted indicator of the average change in the prices as D increases. The sign of the term $\frac{1}{\mu(D)} \cdot \frac{dU}{dD}$ indicates whether utility increases or decreases as a man moves to a location with a higher value of D, and the term itself may be thought of as an indication of the change in real income. Consequently, equation (6) may be rewritten as

$$\Delta \text{ money wage} = \Delta \text{ real income} + \Delta \text{ cost of living.} \qquad (6')$$

Following a terminology introduced into economics by Ohlin,[1] we shall refer to the two components of the right-hand side of equation (6) as 'real' and 'equalizing'. Any income differential can in principle be broken down into real and equalizing components, the latter being the difference, if any, in the cost of living facing people in the countries or sectors compared.

The optimum location $\hat{D}$ is where real income is maximized, that is, where

$$\frac{\mathrm{d}U}{\mathrm{d}D} = \Delta \text{ real income} = 0 \qquad (7)$$

and

$$\frac{\mathrm{d}W(\hat{D})}{\mathrm{d}D} = \sum_i Q_i(\hat{D}) \frac{\mathrm{d}P_i(\hat{D})}{\mathrm{d}D}, \qquad (8)$$

or $\qquad \Delta \text{ money wage} = \Delta \text{ cost of living.} \qquad (8')$

A finite change in location away from $\hat{D}$ lowers real income. At all locations except $\hat{D}$, a change in location alters the wage and the cost of living by different amounts, leaving a residual positive or negative change in real income.[2]

Had he maximized money income instead of utility, the labourer would have located where

$$\Delta \text{ money wage} = 0. \qquad (9)$$

The location satisfying equation (8) does not satisfy equation (9) and vice versa, except when the money wage and the ratio of the money wage and the cost of living reach their maxima at the same place, or when the cost of living is the same everywhere. It is because this last condition (or its equivalent that the market is at a point) is assumed to be true in expositions of economic theory, that the conflict between maximizing money income and maximizing real income at a moment of time does not arise.

The proposition in ordinary economic theory that economic man as a producer maximizes money income, has its geographical

[1] B. Ohlin, *Interregional and International Trade* (1933), p. 212.
[2] Equation (8) is only a first order maximizing condition. The equation also holds for minima and for all local maxima.

counterpart in the proposition that the labourer maximizes real income defined by the index

$$\text{real income} = \frac{W(D) \times 100}{\sum_i P_i(D) Q_i(\hat{D})}, \qquad (10)$$

where the denominator of the fraction may be thought of as a cost of living index at quantity weights of the optimum location. The index of real income reaches its maximum (100) at $\hat{D}$. An important difference between maximization of money income in a one-point economy and maximization of real income in a geographical model is that the former criterion is public and common to the whole market while the latter is private and different from one man to the next. The money wage $W(D)$ is by definition the same for everyone, but the quantity weights in the denominator of the index of real income are derived in part from the utility function, U. People with different utility functions have different optimum locations, different $Q_i(D)$, and different indices of real income; people who like oysters are more likely to live near to the sea.

We now turn our attention from the individual labourer to the labour market. It is convenient to suppose that all labourers have the same tastes so that real income may be disassociated from the tastes of any particular person and considered as a property of the market as a whole. We are also assuming that the labour force cannot cluster at one point but must spread out over the range (O, D^*). This implies that prices and wages must adjust themselves so that equation (8), which was formerly true only at the optimum location $\hat{D}$, is now true at all locations, for no location can be better than the rest in a labour market in equilibrium.

Equation (8), considered as an equilibrium condition of the labour market, can be transformed to show relations among wages, prices, and transport cost (interpreted in this context as any impediments to the free movement of goods). The cost of transporting each good is expressed, not in money, but in terms itself. For instance, the cost of transporting grain is recorded as the number of tons of grain required to pay for the transport of a ton of grain over a distance of one kilometre. The cost of transport of the good i at location D is defined as

$$T_i(D) = \frac{\mathrm{d}P_i(D)}{\mathrm{d}D} \bigg/ P_i, \tag{11}$$

where $T_i(D)$ is positive or negative depending on the direction of trade of the good i at D. Substituting $T_i(D)$ into equation (8) yields the result

$$\frac{\mathrm{d}W(D)}{\mathrm{d}D} = \sum_i Q_i(D)P_i(D)T_i(D) \tag{12}$$

which may be rewritten as

$\varDelta$ money wage $= \sum_i$ (expenditure on i) ($\varDelta$ transport cost of i).   (12')

Wages differ from place to place in a labour market in equilibrium because different amounts of transport services are required to procure identical bundles of goods in different places. The appropriate increment in wages between any two locations is the difference in the transport costs imbedded in equivalent bundles of goods in the two locations.

The important outcome of this analysis from our point of view is that the principle of income maximization no longer obliges us to believe that foreign exchange rates reflect purchasing power parity. Money income may be used to measure real income, welfare, or productivity when prices do not differ very much between the regions in the income comparison. But it should no longer surprise us to find income comparisons of all kinds yielding absurd results when price levels differ considerably from place to place. The theoretical problem of explaining the failure of the purchasing power parity doctrine gives way to the empirical problems of finding out whether there are geographical price differentials and of correcting for them.

This negative result is really enough for our purposes and we could proceed directly to the study of the components of the international and interregional price structure. Instead we shall pause a little longer with the geographical model to bring out a few of its implications about economics generally.

(b) CRITERIA OF MAXIMIZATION IN THE ECONOMY AS A WHOLE

The geographical model was presented in a way that might convey the impression that the maximization of real income replaces the maximization of money income as the sole criterion of behaviour on the supply side of the economy whenever these criteria conflict.

This would be an incorrect inference, for the maximization of real income took precedence over maximization of money income in the model because of a special assumption which is generally true of labour but not always true of other factors of production. The assumption is that labour must work and consume in the same place. This assumption was crucial to the model, for if the labourer could work where wages are high and live where prices are low, he would choose the job with the highest money wage, and we should be back in the familiar textbook world of economic analysis portrayed in Fig. 7(a).

Generalized to apply to all factors of production, this assumption is that income must be consumed where it is earned, that the owner of each factor of production must live and consume where the factor is employed. This expression of the assumption reveals its weakness, for it is not true that the owner of General Motors shares is constrained to live in Detroit. Broadly speaking and with many exceptions, this assumption is true of labour and untrue of the non-human factors of production. The average working man cannot afford to live more than a few miles from his place of work, and he normally makes most of his regular purchases at shops quite near his home even if he knows that prices of some goods are very much lower at other shops a long distance away. On the other hand, the owner of property is not usually constrained to live near his property, for he can arrange for dividends on shares or rent of land to be transferred to him wherever he happens to be. There is nothing incongruous in a resident of Argentina owning and receiving income from property in the United Kingdom, but one is hard put to find examples of a resident of Argentina actually working in the United Kingdom.

Exceptions can easily be found to both sides of this rule. A man may work in the city where wages are high and support his family in the country where prices are low; a man may work in the city and retire to the country; shopping expeditions take one some distance from one's place of work. Equally a business man may be tied to his shop or factory in the same way that a labourer is tied to his place of work, and even a shareholder may allow his choice of residence to be influenced by his intention to attend company meetings. There is a continuum from rigid attachment of the place of residence to the place where one's resources, including labour power, are employed, to a choice of residence unconstrained by the location of one's resources. For our purpose it is convenient to reason in terms of two extremes; the labourer must reside near his place of work, while the owner of property makes his choice of residence independently of where his property is employed.

Our departure from the market at a point in space to a market in a region leads us to the unfortunate situation of having to replace the single, neat criterion, the maximization of money income, with a pair of criteria, one for labour, and one for property. Labour maximizes real income as shown in the preceding section. Property, which may be deployed independently of the location of its owner, is used to maximize money income in the way described in the usual models of economic theory. Even this dual criterion is no more than a convenient simplification, because the labour–property distinction represents poles at the ends of a continuum, and because real income is not objective in the way that money income is objective, for real income is conditioned by characteristics of utility functions that may differ from one man to the next.

(c) IMPLICATIONS ABOUT ECONOMIC THEORY

(1) General equilibrium

In a market at a point, the general equilibrium is specified by three conditions:[1] (a) each economic agent deploys his resources to maximize his money income subject to a given set of prices (including wages); (b) each economic agent maximizes his utility subject to a given income and set of prices; (c) a set of incomes and prices is found that satisfies the preceding conditions simultaneously for all economic agents.

One extra step is required when geography is introduced. To (a) and (b) must be added the qualification 'at each location'. Between (b) and (c) is inserted the condition that each economic agent chooses a location maximizing utility. Condition (c) remains unchanged. This is a sizeable expansion of the general equilibrium model because the revised system requires a statement of the opportunities open to each economic agent at each location.[2]

[1] See for instance G. Debreu, *The Theory of Value*, John Wiley and Sons, 1954, section 6.2.

[2] Among the authors who overlook the fact that some economic agents do not maximize money income in a general equilibrium model with geography are

Of greater theoretical importance than its effect on the size of the general equilibrium model is the fact that the new third step blurs the formerly clear distinction between the supply and demand sides of the economy. At any set of prices, supply and demand may be treated separately at each location, but the final choice of location requires examination of supply and demand together.

(2) The production possibility curve, demand and supply curves, Engel curves, and the consumption function

A direct consequence of the interdependence of supply and demand in a market in a region is the breakdown of the production possibility curve. This curve is well-defined in a market at a point. It ceases to be well-defined when geography is introduced into the economic model.

The production possibility curve is the locus of points representing possible maximum outputs of the commodities in different proportions. These maxima can be specified independently of how the product is distributed because the costs of all distributions are the same (perhaps zero) in a market at a point. In a region, an economy producing two outputs, grain and machines, requires at least three industries, one to produce grain, a second to produce machines, and a third to transport the grain and machines from the places where they are made to the places where they are consumed. The amounts of grain and machines that may be produced in any given proportion are not technically fixed but vary with the amount of society's resources taken up in transport. More of both grain and machines can be produced if consumers of grain tend to live where grain is grown and consumers of machines tend to live were machines are made, than if all consumers take both goods in a fixed proportion. The production possibility curve is no longer

---

G. Debreu, op. cit. (who states on p. 43 of *The Theory of Value* that 'Given the price system *P*, the *j* producer chooses his production in the production set *yj* so as to maximize his profit'); August Losch (see *The Economies of Location*, footnote 6, p. 94), and Walter Isard (see *Location and Space Economy*, equation (45), p. 250). Even B. Ohlin, who seems to be the first to have seriously considered the significance of geographical variation of the price level, constructed a model in which this variation could not occur (see *Interregional and International Trade*, the mathematical statement). The only instance I have been able to find in which income maximization and utility maximization are studied jointly is Louis Lefeber, *Allocation in Space*; see Appendix 4, entitled 'General Equilibrium: Competitive Determination of Market Price Ratios in Geographically Separated Markets'.

unambiguously defined except by imposing assumptions about the demand side of the economy.

Demand and supply curves fare better, and there are important usages of these curves that are not rendered in any degree imprecise by geography. Exact demand or supply curves may be drawn showing the reaction of an economic agent at a fixed location to price changes at that location or to price changes throughout a region if prices may be counted on to rise or fall together in a systematic way. Demand or supply curves cease to be exact, and it ceases to be possible to establish the required one-to-one relation between price and quantity in a region, when these curves are supposed to describe behaviour of people who are able to move about in a region within which prices are not identical, or when prices can vary independently from place to place.

Equalizing differences in income can play queer tricks with Engel curves and consumption functions. The theory of Engel curves is formulated with respect to changes in real income. Engel curves are designed to show how consumption patterns change as people become better off. In measuring Engel curves, consumption of, or expenditure on, a commodity is compared with income, on the implicit assumption that income differentials are real. Should an income differential be equalizing, if a difference in income is matched by a difference in the price level, then the income differential has no effect on the amount of a commodity consumed. Thus cross-section data on a population in which income differentials are equalizing rather than real, yield income elasticities clustering around zero respect to amounts and clustering around one with respect to values of all commodities; deviations from zero and one respectively are due entirely to the accidental effects of price changes and not at all to the phenomena that Engel curves are designed to record. If income differentials among people are partly equalizing and partly real, cross-section data yields biased estimates of the real income elasticities. An identical bias may arise in measuring a consumption function from cross-section data. Cross-section data on a population for which income differentials are equalizing would generate a consumption function that is a straight line through the origin, but this function would carry no implications about comparative saving patterns of rich and poor people because the function is constructed from data pertaining to people all equally well off; the observations are in fact disguised replications of a single observation.

(d) APPLICATION TO PUBLIC FINANCE

We have so far attempted to show the effects of geography on some of the tools of economic analysis Now we try to demonstrate a few of the ways in which economic reasoning based on an economy at a point can be misleading when applied to an economy in which price levels differ from place to place. Three issues are examined in turn: Marshall's case for a progressive income tax, the possibility of increasing total real income through redistribution of money income, and cost-benefit analysis.

(1) Marshall's case for a progressive income tax

Despite the scepticism among economists about interpersonal comparison of utility, Marshall's case for a progressive income tax carries a certain force, and it seems worth-while pointing out that his argument, which is valid in a market at a point, might become invalid in a region where prices differ from place to place. Marshall assumed that the object of tax policy is to get a certain amount of public revenue in a way that leaves the sum of all men's utilities as large as possible, that the relation between income and utility is the same for everyone and that there is a diminishing marginal utility of income. On these assumptions, he shows that an income tax ought to be progressive.

Hidden in the argument is the assumption, which is true only of a market at a point, that real income and money income are identical, that any and all dollars exercise the same degree of command over goods and services. We have shown how this assumption might be false. Should a small money income correspond to a low price level rather than to a low real income, the marginal utility of real income need not be high when money income is low, and the essential step in Marshall's argument becomes invalid.

Oddly enough, the case for a progressive income tax can be restored on somewhat different lines. Suppose that, as in equation (8) of Section (a) above, money incomes differ among people even though real incomes are the same. Now the progressive income tax might maximize total utility by producing an inequality of income. The marginal utility of money is low in high income areas, not because real income is large, but because money represents a relatively small amount of real income. Total utility of the community can be increased by concentrating utility in the area where prices are low. The utility of the community is maximized when the impoverishment of people in the high price areas has reached a point where their lower utility of money due to the high price level is balanced by a greater marginal utility of money due to their reduced real incomes. The argument that a progressive income tax can maximize total utility of the community by fostering inequality requires as a premise that labour is relatively immobile. Should labour be able to move from place to place in response to a tax system, it would reallocate itself among possible locations to equalize post-tax income everywhere. It may be shown that only a proportional income tax maximizes total welfare in this case.

(2) Increasing total real income through redistribution

When differences in income are wholly or partly equalizing, there arises the possibility of increasing the total real income by transferring money from people in high price areas to people in low price areas. As, by definition, a dollar buys more goods and services in low price areas than in high price areas, the transfer of purchasing power between the areas can increase total amounts of goods and services available. The extra income comes from a saving in transport cost. The main reason why prices are higher in some areas than in others, is that certain areas absorb a disproportionate amount of transport cost. The difference in price levels is a rough measure of the resources released from transport to production when purchasing power is transferred from one area to another.

This odd possibility of increasing real income through redistribution of money income may on occasion be realized in foreign aid. Many recipient countries have lower price levels than donor countries. Consequently a direct grant provides the recipient country with a larger real income than it takes from the donor country. As the discrepancy between price levels may be several hundred per cent and may vary considerably among the recipient countries, a policy of giving aid 'where it does the most good' ought to make allowance for price levels if success is to be measured by a financial criterion. An investment in a low price area may generate a great deal of real income even though it yields a low return in money terms.

(3) Cost-benefit analysis

Cost-benefit analysis is a particular case of the rule of thumb in public finance that the object of tax and expenditure policy is to maximize national income, or rather, the present value of the stream of national income, with incomes accruing in different years compared by a time-structure of interest rates.

Maximization of national income as a public goal is a generalization of maximization of private income as a goal of the individual. We have seen that this picture of individual behaviour is an oversimplification except in a market at a point. In a market in a region, labour maximizes real income and property maximizes money income. There now arises the question of which income, real or money, ought to be maximized by the public sector. Which of two projects—one yielding higher income in money terms, and another (with benefits accruing in low prices areas) yielding greater benefits in real terms—ought the public authority to prefer?

There are two important cases in which a comparison in money terms is appropriate. The first is when costs are incurred and benefits accrue in the same place. The second case occurs when the public authority is either satisfied with the present distribution of income or is already redistributing income in what it believes to be the optimal way. To be satisfied with the distribution of income, the public authority must attribute the same social significance to a marginal dollar's worth of goods at every location, and this implies that a project that increases income in one location by more than it decreases income elsewhere would make the country as a whole better off.

These two cases cover most instances where cost-benefit analysis is applied. There are, however, occasions when comparisons in real terms would seem to be appropriate. Some countries and all international organizations have jurisdiction over areas where price levels differ significantly from place to place, and where a decision-maker feels that the appropriate distribution of income has not been achieved. We cite once again the example of aid-giving mentioned above in connection with the redistribution of income. It may happen that projects in urban areas appear beneficial because the high urban price level puts a high weighting on benefits.

To sum up, an analogy may be drawn between geographical and temporal variations in the price level. The error in treating income differentials between sectors at a moment of time as necessarily real is the same as the error in treating income differentials over time as necessarily real. Both involve money illusion. One error is to ignore equalizing differences and the other is to ignore inflation. The source of geographical money illusion in that economic theory is normally studied in a model of a world at a point in which the distinction between money income and real income cannot arise. We have shown that the assumption of the world at a point is deep in economic analysis in the sense that many of the tools of economic analysis depend on it. For most practical purposes the assumption of a market at a point does little violence to the facts because geographical price variation is not large. We have pointed out a few cases in which geographical price variation ought to be considered. It happens that this book is about the one topic for which the assumed market at a point simply will not do.

8

The Pricing of Products that do not Enter into International Trade

IN this chapter and in the next three chapters, we examine reasons why comparison of incomes in money terms yields biased indicators of economic welfare, why exchange rates do not conform to purchasing power parity, and why price levels often differ significantly from place to place. Since price levels are averages of prices, the explanation of why price levels differ must lie in the forces causing individual prices to differ from place to place. As summarized in Fig. 6, Chapter 6, these are the pricing of untraded products, international transport cost, internal transport and distribution cost, and tariffs. These four forces are to be examined in turn, and it will be shown how each force, separately or in combination with others, may be a source of bias in income comparisons.

Special care will be taken in stating assumptions about geography and transport cost because these assumptions are fundamental to the analysis and because they are altered from chapter to chapter. The geography of the model is a pair of points in the study of international transport cost, a plain in the study of internal transport cost, and a single point in the study of tariffs. This is not contradictory because the models refer to different stages of trade; international trade may be thought of as taking place between the capital cities of countries while the internal trade covers areas of territory, and tariffs are levied at a single location.

Pricing of untraded[1] goods is a source of bias in comparisons of

---

[1] 'Untraded' in this context refers to goods that do not enter into international trade, presumably because the transport cost is prohibitive. Goods that are untraded in this sense are of course traded in local markets.

money income because the process of trade tends to establish a purchasing power parity among traded goods only. Each country has its own rate of exchange between traded and untraded goods. A country with a comparative advantage in untraded products, tends to place low values on these products, giving them low weights in an income comparison in which quantities are weighted by prices. The rules for computing national income fail to differentiate between a country where untraded products are scarce and expensive, and a country where they are plentiful and cheap. This source of bias may be especially important in comparisons between rich industrial countries and poor agricultural countries, for there is reason to believe that poor agricultural countries have a substantial comparative advantage in untraded products.

Imagine an international economy consisting of many countries located at points, and two distinct kinds of commodities: traded commodities that can be moved costlessly from one country to another and untraded commodities that must be consumed where they are produced. All countries use the same currency, and there are no restrictions on movements of currency or goods across national frontiers. There must be at least two varieties of traded commodities if international trade is to take place, but all of the traded commodities can be amalgamated into a single commodity which we shall call 'goods'. The separate commodities included in 'goods' are weighted by market prices that are forced to be the same in all countries by the assumption that transport is free. It is also assumed that there is only one kind of untraded commodity, called 'services'. This assumption enables the analysis to be compressed into a two-commodity world and illustrated on a two-dimensional diagram.

An income comparison in money terms is made between two countries, Thailand and the U.K. Their populations are assumed to be the same so that any comparison of total income is a comparison of income per head as well. Tastes in the two countries are identical and may be summarized in a common set of community indifference curves. The countries differ in their production possibilities; U.K. is relatively more efficient at producing goods and Thailand is relatively more efficient at producing services.

The income comparison is illustrated on Fig. 8. The axes

indicate amounts of goods and services, the production possibility curves of Thailand and the U.K. are R_T and R_U, outputs on R_T and R_U chosen by Thailand and the U.K. are labelled T and U, and the lines UY_{UU} and TY_{TT} are budget constraints. It is convenient to suppose that these outputs lie on the same indifference curve. This final assumption, which is not really

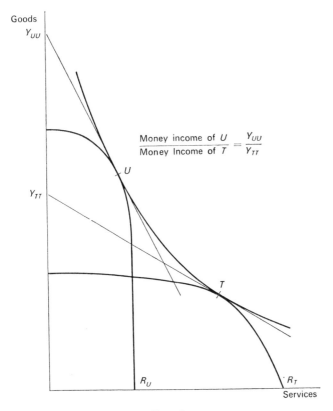

$$\frac{\text{Money income of } U}{\text{Money income of } T} = \frac{Y_{UU}}{Y_{TT}}$$

FIG. 8

necessary and which will be relaxed presently, allows bias in the income comparison to be assessed with reference to an indifference curve rather than with reference to the binary comparisons. Thailand's comparative advantage in services and the comparative advantage of the U.K. in goods are reflected in the slopes of the production possibility curves. R_U is steeper than R_T at any proportion between outputs of goods and services. As the figure shows,

7

people in the U.K. consume a comparatively high proportion of goods to services because goods are relatively cheap in the U.K., and people in Thailand consume a comparatively low proportion of goods to services because goods are relatively expensive in Thailand.

The next step in the argument is to transform quantities and relative prices into money incomes. The transition is particularly simple in this model because goods are costless to transport. If all countries use the same currency and goods are costless to transport, then arbitrage ensures that the price of goods is the same everywhere, and goods themselves may serve as an international monetary standard.

The national incomes of Thailand and the U.K. evaluated in goods at local relative prices are Y_{TT} and Y_{UU}. We do not, of course, know the values of the national incomes in baht or £, but we do know that the ratio of national incomes in baht or £ is equal to the ratio of these incomes measured in amounts of 'goods', i.e. the ratio of the national incomes of the U.K. and Thailand is Y_{UU}/Y_{TT}. It follows directly from the convexity of the indifference curve that $Y_{UU} > Y_{TT}$; the country consuming the larger proportion of goods has the higher national income and appears to be better off. The convexity of the indifference curve at once assures that if the real incomes of Thailand and the U.K. are the same, the money income of the U.K. is greater than the money income of Thailand.

The argument can be stated in more formal terms. The definitions of money incomes are

$$Y_{U£} = P_{GU}Q_{GU} + P_{SU}Q_{SU},$$
$$Y_{T\,baht} = P_{GT}Q_{GT} + P_{ST}Q_{ST},$$

where $Y_{U£}$ and $Y_{T\,baht}$ are money national incomes, P and Q are prices and quantities, and the subscripts refer to countries and commodities in the obvious way. Since both countries use the same currency and goods are costless to transport

$$P_{GU} = P_{GT}.$$

The ratio of money incomes is

$$\frac{Y_{U£}}{Y_{T\,baht}} = \frac{P_{GU}}{P_{GT}} \cdot \frac{Q_{GU} + \dfrac{P_{SU}}{P_{GU}}Q_{SU}}{Q_{GT} + \dfrac{P_{ST}}{P_{GT}}Q_{ST}} = \frac{P_{GU}}{P_{GT}} \cdot \frac{Y_{UU}}{Y_{TT}} = \frac{Y_{UU}}{Y_{TT}}.$$

The source of the bias is revealed by this equation to be the fact that the comparison of money incomes weights the untraded product of each country at its own relative price in relation to the traded product (P_{SU}/P_{GU} and P_{ST}/P_{GT}), instead of at one single price common to both countries. The bias goes against Thailand,

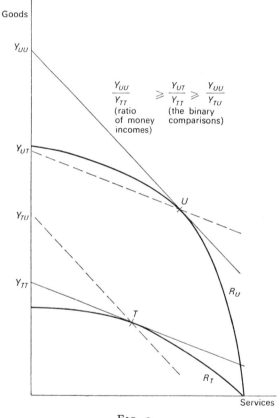

$$\frac{Y_{UU}}{Y_{TT}} \geqslant \frac{Y_{UT}}{Y_{TT}} \geqslant \frac{Y_{UU}}{Y_{TU}}$$

(ratio of money incomes)   (the binary comparisons)

FIG. 9

the country with the comparative advantage in untraded products, because the international price mechanism establishes a purchasing power parity in traded products only.

In the more general case where consumption patterns do not lie on the same indifference curve, the bias in the comparison of money incomes as an indicator of comparative welfare is assessed from the binary comparisons. Figs. 8 and 9 are alike except in the shapes of the production possibility curves. Fig. 9 is drawn to show two countries equally efficient at producing services that do not enter into international trade, but unequal in efficiency in producing tradable goods. The outputs of the U.K. and of Thailand would be equal if both countries confined themselves to producing services. But the U.K. can produce more goods and has the higher marginal rate of trade-off in production between goods and services for any given output of services.

As in Fig. 8, ratios of money may be read off the vertical axis. Once again the comparison of money incomes is $\dfrac{Y_{UU}}{Y_{TT}}$. The binary comparisons are $\dfrac{Y_{UU}}{Y_{TU}}$ and $\dfrac{Y_{UT}}{Y_{TT}}$, which are both smaller than $\dfrac{Y_{UU}}{Y_{TT}}$, for $Y_{TU} \geqslant Y_{TT}$ and $Y_{UT} \leqslant Y_{UU}$ when each country consumes the larger proportion of the good in which it has a comparative advantage. The comparison of money incomes is necessarily outside the range of the binary comparisons.

The case described in Fig. 9 is sometimes representative of comparisons between developed and underdeveloped countries. 'Services' may be thought of literally, as services rendered directly from one man to another without the intermediary of tangible physical goods. Services include public administration, domestic service, religion, medicine, law, restaurants, barbers, laundries, distribution of goods, etc. Economic progress is primarily the development of efficiency in the production of tangible physical goods, and the developed country is developed in virtue of its greater capacity to produce these things. Tangible physical goods are comparatively cheap in developed countries and comparatively dear in underdeveloped countries. Tangible physical goods are tradable internationally but services are not. Consequently the price mechanism biases down incomes of underdeveloped countries by valuing untraded products at local prices, rather than on a common scale as would be required of a proper welfare comparison. Incomes of underdeveloped countries appear low because untraded products are cheap.

An important special case of untraded products is distribution. All commodities purchased retail are in a sense joint products of industry and trade, that is, of production at the work bench, factory, or farm, and of distribution from places where products are made to places where they may be bought by final consumers. In the context of an income comparison among countries, trade, including local transport and wholesale and retail distribution, is itself an untradable product. Local distribution must, by definition, be done locally. Hence, income is biased down where local transport and distribution are cheap.

The evidence in Part III, though limited in scope, suggests that transport and distribution are comparatively cheap in poor countries. There is reason to expect this to be so. Technical progress seems to have impinged less on distribution that on production. The English shopkeeper today does not seem to be markedly more efficient at distributing goods than the English shopkeeper of the eighteenth century or the typical shopkeeper in the underdeveloped countries today. There have been innovations in distribution, but the contrast between the corner grocery and the supermarket is hardly comparable to that between the handloom and the modern clothing factory. Because developed countries have a comparative advantage in production as compared with distribution, the services of distribution must be relatively expensive in the developed countries, when wages equalize among lines of work. Consequently, the spread between the international price of any commodity and its local retail price is greater in developed than in underdeveloped countries, and incomes of developed countries are buoyed up accordingly.

9

International Transport Cost

INCOME in any country, region, or sector is buoyed up by the transport cost in goods and services consumed there. Money income must be relatively high in a mining camp where most items of consumption are imported, and relatively low in a largely self-sufficient farming district if people in both places are equally prosperous. Similarly, transport and distribution cost can cause money income to be high in an industrial country and low in an agricultural country if real incomes in these countries are the same. It is often supposed in discussion of purchasing power parity that, as there are transport costs in both exports and imports of any country, the highs and lows of prices should balance off among countries leaving price levels more or less the same everywhere. In this chapter it will be shown how this tendency toward equalization of price levels may stop well short of actual equality.

Again, as in Chapter 8, we suppose that world prices are established as part of the general equilibrium in international trade. Prices are given, not in the sense that they are established outside the system we are considering, but in that we begin to examine the system after prices are generated. A new aspect of the international price structure enters the analysis on abandoning the assumption that all traded commodities are costless to transport. That assumption made it possible to suppose that each product had a unique world price. Now we must suppose that each product entering into international trade has its own price in each country and that the prices in different countries are related by the rule that the spreads between prices of identical products in different places cannot exceed the cost of transport. If a product sells for £2 in the U.K. and if it may be transported from the U.K.

to Thailand at a cost of £1, then the Thai price cannot exceed £3. The Thai price may be less than £3, in which case the product is not exported from the U.K. to Thailand.

A bias in income resulting from international transport cost is illustrated in Fig. 10. The example is of trade among three countries, Thailand, the U.K. and another country. Thailand produces three tons of grain; the U.K. produces two machines; a third country has no physical output but earns income from transport.

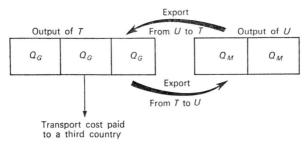

FIG. 10

Transport of machines is free, and the cost of transporting grain is one-half of the quantity dispatched from the port at Thailand. Suppose that trade is in equilibrium when Thailand exports two tons of grain to the U.K. in return for one machine. The U.K. receives only one of the two tons of grain dispatched from Thailand because the other ton accrues to the third country as transport cost. It is convenient to suppose that people in the third country consume only grain, for then Thailand and the U.K. may have identical consumption patterns consisting of one ton of grain and one machine.

We have a complete description of relative prices, outputs, and trade in this simple system. A unit of currency and one money price are the only additional pieces of information needed to compute money incomes. Suppose the world currency is £ and the price of a machine in Thailand is £1. The other three prices may be deduced from the assumptions in this example:

(a) The price of a machine in the U.K. is also £1 because machines are costless to transport.

(b) The price of grain in the U.K. is £1 per ton because one ton of grain is exchanged for one machine in the U.K. and values of exports and imports of the U.K. must be the same.

(c) The price of grain in Thailand is only £0·5 because two tons of grain were exchanged for one machine (worth £1 in Thailand) and the values of the Thai exports and imports must be the same.

These prices are consistent with a balance of trade at both ports. Quantities exported and imported are different in Thailand and the U.K., but money values are the same. Each country buys £1 worth from the other.

The national income of Thailand is £1·5, the value at local prices of the Thai output (three tons of grain), or of Thai consumption (one machine and one ton of grain). The national income of the U.K. is £2, the value at local prices of U.K. output (two machines), or of U.K. consumption (one machine and one ton of grain). The U.K. appears better off than Thailand even though their consumption patterns are identical. The origin of the bias is the transport cost. The amount of the bias is £0·5, the cost of transport that the English must pay and the Thai are able to avoid in the process of consuming grain.

This simple example is sufficient to demonstrate that international transport cost might bias the income comparison in money terms. A model similar to that of the last chapter is used to show when international transport cost biases income comparison and when it does not. The difference between the models is in assumptions about transport cost. In the model of the last chapter, one commodity could be transported free and the other could not be transported at all. Now both commodities can be transported at a cost. It will be shown that the comparison of money incomes is an average of the binary comparisons if and only if transport costs balance out in the sense that some weighted average of the consumption patterns of the two countries costs the same in both countries.

This proposition is illustrated in Fig. 11. Once again the points T and U refer to the consumption patterns of Thailand and the U.K. in a two commodity economy. Relative prices in Thailand and the U.K. are indicated by the slopes of the unbroken straight lines $T\overline{T}$ and $U\overline{U}$. The price differential between Thailand and the U.K. is due to transport cost in foreign trade. The relative price of grain is low in Thailand because Thailand exports grain to the U.K. and imports machines. No assumption need be made about the amount of trade with third countries. We could as well suppose that Thailand and the U.K. trade only with each other, or that they are imbedded in a multilateral system of international trade. The straight lines, N_T and N_U, drawn from the origin through the points T and U, contain all points representing

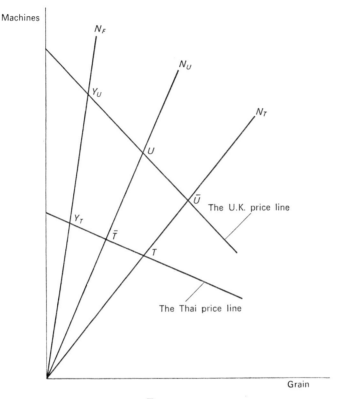

FIG. 11

bundles of grain and machines in the proportions consumed in Thailand and the U.K. respectively.

The binary comparisons, ratios of the incomes in the U.K. and Thailand at U.K. and Thai prices respectively, are indicated on the diagram by the ratios $O\overline{U}/OT$ and $OU/O\overline{T}$ where O is the origin of the diagram and U and T are the intersections of the budget constraints through U and T with lines N_T and N_U. The binary comparisons have been illustrated in earlier diagrams of this type by projecting the point U and T along parallel budget constraints onto the vertical axis. The choice of the vertical axis in this construction was arbitrary because the same ratio of the incomes of the U.K. and Thailand at a common set of prices would result from projecting the points U and T on to the horizontal axis or on to any other straight line passing through the origin of the diagram. (This statement follows from the proposition in geometry that a line parallel to the base of a triangle cuts the other two sides in equal proportions.) In particular, ratios of the incomes of the U.K. and Thailand at a common set of prices could be measured as distances from the origin on the line N_U or on the line N_T. We choose to measure the ratio of incomes of the U.K. and Thailand by projecting the points U and T onto the line N_T, using budget constraints sloped according to the relative price of grain and machines in the U.K. The projections of U and T onto N_T are $\bar{U}$ and T. If the points U and T were projected onto the vertical axis the intersections would be Y_{UU} and Y_{TU} as shown in Figure 9, and the ratio of the U.K. and Thai incomes would be Y_{UU}/Y_{TU}. The ratio $O\bar{U}/OT$ is exactly equal to the ratio Y_{UU}/Y_{TU}. Therefore, $O\bar{U}/OT$ must be the ratio of incomes of the U.K. and Thailand at U.K. prices. Similarly, $OU/O\bar{T}$ is the ratio of the incomes of the U.K. and Thailand at Thai prices.

The next and most important step is to put comparisons of money income on to the diagram. This can be done with an exceedingly simple construction, but one that requires some justification. If machines were costless to transport the price of machines would be the same everywhere, money values would be proportional to values expressed in numbers of machines, and ratios of money incomes could be indicated as ratios of distances on the vertical axis in the same way and for the same reasons as in the preceding chapter. Similarly if grain were costless to transport and machines were not, ratios of money incomes in the U.K. and Thailand could be measured as ratios of distances on the horizontal axis. This suggests that when neither good is costless to transport, money incomes may be represented as distances on a line through the origin somewhere between the extremes of the horizontal and vertical axis.

When both goods are costly to transport, and when, as is being assumed, the import of each country is the export of the other, it becomes possible to find a composite good that costs the same in both countries. Since the U.K. exports machines and Thailand exports grain, the prices of the two goods in the U.K. and Thailand are related by the formulae

$$P_{MT} = P_{MU}(1+T_M)$$

and

$$P_{GU} = P_{GT}(1+T_G),$$

where P is price and T_G and T_M are the transport costs of grain and machines respectively, expressed as percentages of prices in the exporting countries. Suppose that the composite good that costs the same in both countries contains $\overline{Q}_M$ machines and $\overline{Q}_G$ tons of grain. Since the composite good $(\overline{Q}_M, \overline{Q}_G)$ costs the same in the two countries

$$\overline{Q}_M P_{MU} + \overline{Q}_G P_{GU} = \overline{Q}_M P_{MT} + \overline{Q}_G P_{GT}$$

so that

$$\overline{Q}_M P_{MU} + \overline{Q}_G P_{GT}(1+T_G) = \overline{Q}_M P_{MU}(1+T_M) + \overline{Q}_G P_{GT}.$$

Therefore

$$\overline{Q}_G P_{GT} T_G = \overline{Q}_M P_{MU} T_M$$

and

$$\frac{\overline{Q}_G}{\overline{Q}_M} = \frac{P_{MU} T_M}{P_{GT} T_G}.$$

The proportions of grain and machines in the composite commodity costing the same in both countries is the inverse of the ratio of their costs of transport, $P_{MU}T_M/P_{GT}T_G$.

Bundles of grain and machines in this proportion are indicated in the diagram by the line N_F, locus of all bundles of goods that have the same price in both countries. The line N_F may in principle lie anywhere between the vertical and horizontal axis depending on which good is the more costly to transport. If machines are relatively cheap to transport and grain relatively costly, the line N_F tends to lie close to the vertical axis; when machines may be transported costlessly, N_F must be the vertical axis unless grain is also costless to transport, in which case N_F is not defined.

Distances along the line N_F may now serve to measure money incomes in the same way that distances along the vertical axis were used in the last chapter. Since bundles of goods on N_F have the same value in Thailand and the U.K., the ratios of money incomes at local prices in Thailand and the U.K. are proportional to the ratios of the bundles of goods on N_F that the incomes of Thailand and the U.K. can buy. The ratio of money incomes of the U.K. and Thailand is shown in Fig. 11 as the fraction $\dfrac{OY_U}{OY_T}$ where Y_U and Y_T are the intersections with N_F of the budget constraints $U\overline{U}$ and $T\overline{T}$ of the U.K. and Thailand respectively.

The relation we have been deriving among transport costs, the binary comparisons and the comparison of money incomes, can now be read off Fig. 11. Imagine the line N_F swinging clockwise from a position on the vertical axis through the north-east quadrant until it reaches the horizontal axis. Since the line $U\overline{U}$ is steeper than the line $T\overline{T}$, the clockwise rotation of N_F causes the ratio OY_U/OY_T to decrease steadily from a maximum when N_F is vertical to a minimum when N_F is horizontal. When N_F reaches N_U, the points Y_U and Y_T take up the positions U and $\overline{T}$, indicating that the ratio of money incomes is equal to $OU/O\overline{T}$, the binary comparison at Thai prices. When N_F reaches N_T, the points Y_U and Y_T take up the positions $\overline{U}$ and T, indicating that the ratio of money incomes is equal to $O\overline{U}/OT$, the binary comparison at U.K. prices. Consequently the ratio of money incomes is larger than either binary comparison

$$\frac{OY_U}{OY_T} \geqslant \frac{OU}{O\overline{T}} \geqslant \frac{O\overline{U}}{OT}$$

when N_F is to the left of N_U; it is between the binary comparisons

$$\frac{OU}{O\overline{T}} \geqslant \frac{OY_U}{OY_T} \geqslant \frac{O\overline{U}}{OT}$$

when N_F is between N_U and N_T; it is less than either binary comparison

$$\frac{OU}{O\overline{T}} \geqslant \frac{O\overline{U}}{OT} \geqslant \frac{OY_U}{OY_T}$$

when N_F is to the right of N_T.

The rule has a simple economic interpretation. The income of Thailand appears smaller by comparison with the income of the U.K., the steeper the line N_F and flatter the lines N_U and N_T. The line N_F is steep when the Thai export is expensive to transport in comparison with the U.K. export. The lines N_U and N_T tend to be flat when the type of good exported by Thailand constitutes a large proportion of consumption. Thus the income of Thailand appears smaller the greater the cost of transport of its exports, the less the cost of transport of its imports, and the larger the share of the types of commodities it exports in the total value of consumption. The ratio of the money incomes of Thailand and the U.K. is spanned by the binary comparisons when N_F is spanned by N_U and N_T, that is, when transport cost in imported goods buoys up the incomes of the U.K. and Thailand to about the same extent, when highs and lows of prices balance off in the sense that an average of the consumption patterns in the two countries has the same money value in both.

A significant feature of this demonstration is that it contains no assumption about the volume of trade. The bias due to transport cost depends exclusively on a relation between consumption patterns, transport costs, and relative prices in the two countries.

Comparing Thailand and the U.K. as real countries, rather than as fictional ones in an example, it seems reasonable to suppose that international transport cost would bias down the income of Thailand because Thailand's main export is rice which is somewhat expensive to transport and which is, or is a substitute for, a fair proportion of consumption in Thailand and the U.K. But the bias in transport cost is not uniformly against underdeveloped countries or suppliers of primary material. If country T exports iron to country U in return for cars, and if both countries consume the same number of cars, cars being the only consumption good, the comparison of incomes of countries U and T in money terms makes country T seem to have the higher real income. The income of an exporter of an industrial raw material which is expensive to transport in relation to its value at the home port is not biased down in international trade because the product does not enter into consumption. The incomes of the oil-exporting countries may not be biased down because oil constitutes a small share of the value of the consumption of the country producing it.

Biases in income caused by the pricing of untraded goods, discussed in Chapter 8, and by asymmetrical transport and distribution cost, are cumulative. Imagine Fig. 11 as a projection from above of a slice of a three-dimensional diagram in which the vertical axis represents untraded goods. The budget constraints at U and T become tangent plains to three dimensional production possibility curves. In each country, relative prices of traded and untraded goods are the slopes of the plains toward the vertical axis. The money price of untraded goods is equal to the money price of traded goods times the rate of transformation in production between traded and untraded goods. Any force that biases down the average price of traded goods, biases down the price of untraded goods as well.

10

Domestic Transport Cost

THE influence of domestic transport cost on the measurement of productivity is so similar to the influence of international transport cost on the measurement of national income that the apparatus developed in the last two chapters could easily be put to work here. The two-point world, with each point representing a country, would be replaced by a two-point country, with each point representing the location of an industry, and all of the results in the last chapter would have their counterparts about productivity measurement. Partly because the application of the apparatus of the last chapter to domestic transport cost is so straightforward that the reader can at once imagine all the results, and partly because an alternative apparatus leads to some interesting theory, we now abandon the two-point world and proceed to a genuine two-dimensional geography in which distance as opposed to mere location plays some part.

THE ASSUMPTIONS AND THE DEFINITIONS OF VARIABLES

The model is built on five blocks of assumptions.

(1) Geography

There is a disc-shaped country, with a city in the centre and farmland of uniform quality everywhere else. This is the simplest of all possible two-dimensional geographies because it allows location to be indicated by a single variable, D, the distance from the city, instead of by two variables like latitude and longitude; circular symmetry assures that any economic activity taking place at any point on a ring a given distance from the city is also taking place at every other point on that ring. The location of the city is designated as the point $D = 0$ and the radius of the country is D^*.

Variables dependent on location are usually identified as functions of D, but they may be written without D if the meaning is clear or if a variable that could in principle depend on D is, in fact, constant with respect to location.

(2) Production

Grain is the only commodity. The production function is

$$O = El^\alpha \tag{1}$$

where O is output per unit area, l is the labour employed per unit area, and E and α are technical constants. This is a Cobb-Douglas production function. Land does not enter explicitly into equation (1), because the variables are defined per unit area.

(3) Population

The population consists of S landlords and L workers. Landlords live and consume in the city. Workers divide themselves into L_F farm workers, and L_T transport workers who carry the landlords' share of the grain from the farms to the city. All workers are equally skilled, there is free mobility between occupations and among locations in search of jobs, all workers must work and consume at the same place, and each worker strives to maximize his real income in grain. Consequently, the equilibrium of the system requires that all workers, at all locations and in all occupations, enjoy the same real income in grain.

Landlords are constrained to live in the city as a justification for placing transport workers in the model. If an explanation is required within the economics of the model as to why landlords choose to live in the city when they might enjoy larger real incomes by living on farms where grain is cheap, it might be supposed that landlords act as civil servants, or that they like each other's company, or that they congregate for purposes of defence against the peasants, like the Norman conquerors in their castles. But the real justification for constraining landlords to live in cities is that this case is a simplified representation of the fact that the location of natural resources in a country and the need to cluster certain economic activities in cities, requires that an economy employ transport workers to bring products from the places where they are made to the places where they are consumed.

A model with farm workers and landlords at the farms, and manufacturing undertaken in the city, might yield more satisfactory economics, but as an appendix to this chapter will show, it generates some moderately complex mathematics that does not easily yield exact numerical solutions. Comparing the assumptions of this chapter with those of Chapter 9, it is as if we have bought the two-dimensional geography and the inclusion of transport workers into the model at the price of reducing the number of commodities from two to one. This model of domestic transport can be made consistent with the model of international trade in Chapter 9 by supposing that the landlords trade some of their grain for manufactures produced in other countries.

(4) Transport

Labour is the only factor of production in transport, and the cost of transport, β, is measured in man-years per ton kilometre. To locate transport workers on the scale D, it is supposed that transport workers are stationary and that grain transported from the farm to the city is passed from hand to hand like buckets of water to a fire. Money is costless to transport in the sense that a £ at any location may be exchanged for a £ at any other location.

(5) Prices

The price of grain in the city $P(o)$ is assumed to be £50 per metric ton. Prices $P(D)$ and money wages $W(D)$ at all other locations, D, are determined within the model. The model could have been made slightly more realistic by setting the quantity of money, assuming a velocity of money, and allowing all prices, including the price of grain in the city, to be determined within the model.

The seven parameters D^* (the radius of the country), l and E (properties of the production function), β (the cost of transport), $P(o)$ (the price of grain in the city), L (the labour force), and S (the number of landlords) are sufficient, together with equations derived below, to generate values of all of the variables in the model. The model is therefore a complete general equilibrium. It is however static in that equilibrium values once attained are maintained indefinitely and nothing is said about how the system adjusts in the process of attaining equilibrium.

In addition to D (location), O and l, (output of grain and input of labour per unit area), L_F and L_T (labour force in farming and in

8

transport), $P(D)$ and $W(D)$ (the price of grain and the wage of labour at D), all defined above, the model makes use of the following variables:

C, the real wage of labour in tons of grain per year;

T, defined as $C\beta$, or the cost of transport in tons of grain per ton kilometre;

G, total output of grain, consisting of

G_F consumed by farm workers,

G_T consumed by transport workers,

G_S consumed by landlords;

Y, the national income in £ consisting of

Y_F accruing to farm workers,

Y_S accruing to landlords,

Y_T accruing to transport workers.

THE OUTPUT OF GRAIN

The total output of grain, equal to the output per unit area multiplied by the area of the country,

$$G = \pi D^{*2}O, \tag{2a}$$

$$G = \pi D^{*2}El^{\alpha}, \tag{2b}$$

is divided among the three social classes.

$$G = G_F + G_T + G_S. \tag{3}$$

The real wage in grain is equal to the marginal product of labour on the farm, the derivative of O in equation (1) with respect to l

$$C = \frac{dO}{dl} = \frac{\alpha O}{l}. \tag{4}$$

Since labour is mobile among locations, the real wage, C, must be, independent of location. Equation (4) then implies that l is also independent of location. The farm workers' share of the total output is equal to α.

$$G_F = \alpha G. \tag{5}$$

Since real wages are the same in both occupations,

$$G_T = G_F \frac{L_T}{L_F}. \tag{6}$$

PRICES AND WAGES

The money wage at each location is equal to the value of the real wage.

$$W(D) = P(D)\ C. \tag{7}$$

The function $P(D)$ may be derived from the cost of transporting grain from D to the city. The cost of transporting a ton of grain from D to $D—\Delta D$ is

$$\beta\ W(D)\ \Delta D \equiv \beta\ C\ P(D)\ \Delta D.$$

The value of a unit of grain in the city is equal to its price at D plus the cost of bringing the grain from D to the city, i.e.

$$P(0) = P(D) + \int_D^0 \beta C P(D) \mathrm{d}D. \tag{7a}$$

The solution to this integral is

$$P(D) = P(0)e^{-TD}, \tag{7b}$$

where $P(0)$ is a parameter and

$$T = \beta C. \tag{8}$$

THE LABOUR FORCE

By definition

$$L = L_T + L_F. \tag{9}$$

Since the density of the farm workers is the same everywhere, the total number of farm workers is the product of the density and the area of the country.

$$L_F = \pi D^{*2}l. \tag{10}$$

The method of calculating the number of transport workers is similar to the method of deriving the price of grain. The landlords' share of the output of grain in a ring of width ΔD a distance D from the city is

$$2\pi D(1—\alpha)O\Delta D$$

and its value is

$$2\pi D(1—\alpha)O\ P(D)\Delta D.$$

Transport workers carry this grain to the city, deducting part of it as their wage. Since arbitrage ensures that the value of the landlords' interest in the grain remains constant throughout the journey to the city, the amount of grain arriving at the city is the value of the grain dispatched divided by the city price,

$$2\pi D(1—\alpha)O\frac{P(D)}{P(0)}\Delta D.$$

The transport workers' share of the grain dispatched from the ring at D is therefore

$$2\pi D(1-\alpha)O\left\{1-\frac{P(D)}{P(o)}\right\}\varDelta D$$

and the total number of transport workers required, L_T, is the sum over all of the rings of the transport workers' share of the grain divided by the real wage in grain

$$L_T = \int_0^{D^*} \frac{1}{C} \cdot 2\pi D(1-\alpha)O\left\{1-\frac{P(D)}{P(o)}\right\}dD$$

$$= 2\pi\left\{\frac{(1-\alpha)}{\alpha}\right\}l\int_0^{D^*} D(1-e^{-TD})dD$$

$$= 2\pi\left(\frac{1-\alpha}{\alpha}\right)l\left(\frac{D^{*2}}{2}+\frac{TD^*e^{-TD^*}+e^{-TD^*}-1}{T^2}\right). \quad (11)$$

THE NATIONAL INCOME

By definition

$$Y = Y_F+Y_T+Y_S. \quad (12)$$

The earnings of farm workers in a ring of width $\varDelta D$ a distance D from the city is the product of the density of farm workers, the area of the ring, and the wage at D. This product is

$$2\pi DlW(D)\varDelta D.$$

Therefore

$$Y_F = \int_0^{D^*} 2\pi DlW(D)dD$$

$$= 2\pi ClP(o)\int_0^{D^*} De^{-TD}dD$$

$$= 2\pi ClP(o)\frac{-TD^*e^{-TD^*}-e^{-TD^*}+1}{T^2}. \quad (13)$$

The income of landlords is the value at city prices of the grain they consume

$$Y_S = G_SP(o). \quad (14a)$$

It is also equal to the landlords' share of the value of output on the farms

$$Y_S = \frac{1-\alpha}{\alpha}Y_F. \quad (14b)$$

The total earnings of transport workers is calculated by adding up the earnings at each location $\overline{D}$ associated with the transport of grain originating at each location D. From a total amount of grain

$$2\pi D(1-\alpha)O\varDelta D$$

dispatched from D an amount

$$2\pi D(1-\alpha)O\frac{P(D)}{P(\overline{D})}\varDelta D$$

is left in the owner's possession at $\overline{D}$, because the value of the owner's interest remains constant throughout the journey to the city. From this amount of grain, the transport workers deduct

$$2\pi D(1-\alpha)O\frac{P(D)}{P(\overline{D})}\varDelta D\beta C\varDelta D$$

tons for transporting the grain from $\overline{D}$ to $\overline{D}-\varDelta\overline{D}$, and the value of this deduction is

$$2\pi D(1-\alpha)O\frac{P(D)}{P(\overline{D})}\beta CP(\overline{D})\varDelta D\varDelta\overline{D}.$$

The sum of the values of all deductions of grain by transport workers at all locations $\overline{D}$ and associated with grain originating at all locations D is

$$Y_T = \int_0^{D*}\int_0^D 2\pi\overline{D}(1-\alpha)O\beta CP(0)e^{-TD}\mathrm{d}\overline{D}\mathrm{d}D$$

$$= 2\pi(1-\alpha)OTP(0)\int_0^{D*} D^2 e^{-TD}\mathrm{d}D$$

$$= 2\pi(1-\alpha)OP(0)\frac{2}{T^2}\left\{1-e^{-TD*}\left(1+TD*+\frac{T^2D*^2}{2}\right)\right\}. \quad (15)$$

The system of equations is easily solved numerically from values of the seven parameters. Equations (1), (8)–(11), (2a), and (4) yield values of O, C, l, T, L_F, L_T, and G, and the rest of the variables may be calculated one at a time. The number of landlords, S, may be set arbitrarily because it does not enter into any of the equations. It is convenient to suppose that all landlords have an equal share of the total rent.

A NUMERICAL EXAMPLE

The effects of transport cost on statistics of productivity, income per man employed, are illustrated by giving numerical values to the parameters and allowing the cost of transport to change when other parameters remain constant.

Suppose that the radius of the country, D^*, is 1000 kilometres and that the parameters E and α in the production function are 100 000 and $\frac{1}{2}$ respectively when output, O, is measured in kilograms of grain per square kilometre per year. The price of grain in the city is £50 per metric ton. The transport cost, β, is given the values of 1×10^{-5}, 2×10^{-5}, 5×10^{-5}, 10×10^{-5}, 25×10^{-5}, 50×10^{-5}, and 100×10^{-5} man-years per ton kilometre. The total labour force is 500 million and the number of landlords is 59·07269 million. This is all the information required to generate values of all the variables in the system. The results are summarized in Table 6.

TABLE 6

Transport Cost and Productivity

(a) $\beta = 1 \times 10^{-5}$; $T = 0·040$ kilo per ton kilometre

	Income (£ million)	Economically-active population (million)	Income per head per year (£)
landlords	95 223	59	1614
farm workers	95 223	487	195
transport workers	2542	13	199
Total	192 988	559	345

$\dfrac{P(D^*)}{P(o)} = 0·96$ $C = 4·015$ tons of grain per year
                     $G = 3·9$ thousand million tons

(b) $\beta = 2 \times 10^{-5}$; $T = 0.08$ kilo per ton kilometre

	Income ($£$ million)	Economically-active population (million)	Income per head per year ($£$)
landlords	91 496	59	1551
farm workers	91 496	475	193
transport workers	4960	25	199
Total	187 952	559	336

$\dfrac{P(D^*)}{P(o)} = 0.92$ $C = 4.066$ tons of grain per year
$G = 3.9$ thousand million tons

(c) $\beta = 5 \times 10^{-5}$; $T =$ kilo per ton kilometre

	Income ($£$ million)	Economically-active population (million)	Income per head per year ($£$)
landlords	81 101	59	1375
farm workers	81 101	443	183
transport workers	11 185	57	195
Total	173 387	559	310

$\dfrac{P(D^*)}{P(o)} = 0.81$ $C = 4.213$ tons of grain per year
$G = 3.7$ thousand million tons

(d) $\beta = 10 \times 10^{-5}$; $T = 0.44$ kilo per ton kilometre

	Income ($£$ million)	Economically-active population (million)	Income per head per year ($£$)
landlords	66 263	59	1123
farm workers	66 263	399	166
transport workers	18 844	101	187
Total	151 370	559	271

$\dfrac{P(D^*)}{P(o)} = 0.64$ $C = 4.434$ tons of grain per year
$G = 3.5$ thousand million tons

(e) $\beta = 25 \times 10^{-5}$; $T = 1.23$ kilos per ton kilometre

	Income ($£$ million)	Economically-active population (million)	Income per head per year ($£$)
landlords	36 770	59	623
farm workers	36 770	325	113
transport workers	26 829	175	153
Total	100 369	559	180

$$\frac{P(D^*)}{P(o)} = 0.29$$

$C = 4.913$ tons of grain per year
$G = 3.2$ thousand million tons

(f) $\beta = 50 \times 10^{-5}$; $T = 2.65$ kilos per ton kilometre

	Income ($£$ million)	Economically-active population (million)	Income per head per year ($£$)
landlords	15 656	59	265
farm workers	15 656	280	56
transport workers	20 847	220	95
Total	51 959	559	92

$$\frac{P(D^*)}{P(o)} = 0.07$$

$C = 5.301$ tons of grain per year
$G = 3.0$ thousand million tons

(g) $\beta = 100 \times 10^{-5}$; $T = 5.5$ kilos per ton kilometre

	Income ($£$ million)	Economically-active population (million)	Income per head per year ($£$)
landlords	4561	59	77
farm workers	4561	258	18
transport workers	8547	242	35
Total	17 669	559	32

$$\frac{P(D^*)}{P(o)} = 0.004$$

C 5.515 tons of grain per year
G 2.8 thousand million tons

The cost of transport is represented at the top of each section of the table in two ways, as man-years per ton kilometre, β, and as kilos of grain per ton kilometre, T. The first representation is a technical parameter in the model. The second must be derived from the model because it depends in part on the real wage. But 'kilo of grain per ton kilometre' is an interesting representation of transport cost because empirical data on transport cost is recorded in this way. For instance, the values of T in (a) and (b), 0·04 and 0·08 respectively, lie on either side of the typical cost of transporting grain long distances by canal boat, and value in (f), 2·65, corresponds roughly to the cost of transport by ox-cart.[1]

Transport cost has a marked effect on the money value of the national income and on the ratio of the productivities of labour in transport and in agriculture. The real, as opposed to monetary, effect of the increase in transport cost, T, from 0·04 to 5·51 is to cause the economy to transfer almost half of its labour force from agriculture into transport, reducing the output of grain by a quarter and reducing the real income of landlords substantially. But the national income falls by nine-tenths, from £188 thousand million to £18 thousand million. The average income of farm workers falls from virtual equality with the average income of transport workers, £199 in (a), to just over one-half, £18 as compared with £35 in (g). The difference in average money incomes of farm workers and transport workers is due to their geographical distributions, transport workers being on the average closer to the city. Farm workers and transport workers have different measured productivities even though their real incomes, C, are exactly the same.

No distinction need be made between the real and money incomes of landlords, because the price of grain in the city where the landlords live, is the same in all of the tables. Consequently the twenty-fold variation in money incomes of landlords between (a) and (g) represents a variation in real income as well. The number of landlords was chosen to make the real incomes of landlords and workers the same in table 6(f). The five-fold differential in that table between money incomes of landlords and farm workers is due

---

[1] A collection of costs of transport by types of vehicles is presented in Table XXX of *The Economics of Subsistence Agriculture* by Colin Clark and M. R. Haswell. The identification in this chapter of values of T with means of transport is based on evidence collected in Thailand and presented in Part III, Chapter 14.

entirely to the price levels and represents no difference in living standards.

Some properties of the example are shown on the accompanying chart. The vertical axes, right and left, are pure numbers, interpreted differently for each of the six functions. The horizontal axis represents transport cost, expressed as β at the bottom of the chart and as T on the top. The association of ranges of values of T with specific means of transport is based on Thai data presented in Chapter 14.[1]

---

[1] Transport costs, originating in baht per ton kilometer, are transformed to kilo per ton kilometer by supposing the average price of grain to be 1·5 baht per kilogram.

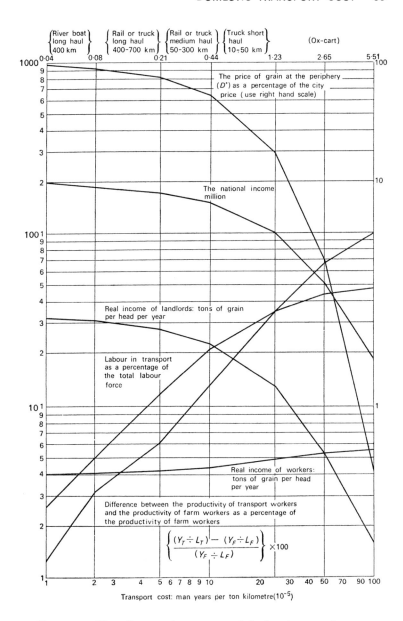

GRAPH I. The effects on the economy of altering the cost of transport.
(Use the left hand scale except when indicated otherwise.)

Appendix I

Placing public expenditure into the model

Suppose that each man, landlord and worker, has to pay a fraction t of his income in grain as tribute to power outside the economic system. The payment of tax requires no extra transport cost because the tax-collectors have a way of receiving the tax at the residence of the tax-payer; landlords pay in the city, farm workers pay at the farm and so on. This is a perfectly neutral tax, for it affects neither the allocation of resources, nor the composition of output, nor the proportional distribution of real net income among the social classes.

Neutrality of this sort is exceptional. In general, the distribution of income among social classes is affected by public expenditure even when this expenditure is financed by an income tax. One might say that the tax is neutral but the expenditure is not. A combination of tax and expenditure is neutral if the tax is used to buy what the tax-payers desist from buying because of the tax, as was assumed to be the case in the paragraph above. The non-neutrality of public expenditure can be demonstrated in an economy at a point in space, but the demonstration is very simple and quite striking in a geographical model, and new attributes of the model are revealed.

We shall contrast two economies identical in every respect except that one economy requires public expenditure to pay civil servants while the other does not. The technical characteristics of these economies, the shapes and areas of the countries and the production functions, are the same as in the principal model of this chapter. In both economies the labour force is 1157 million workers, the cost of transport, is 50×10^{-5} man-years per ton kilometre, the price of grain in the city is £50 a metric ton, and there are 59·0727 million landlords, S, each owning an equal share of the total rent. Economy A requires 378 million civil servants who must live in the city, and its net labour force available for work on farms or in transport is 779 million workers. Economy B can devote all of its 1157 million workers to farming or transport.

Some new variables are required for economy A and some equations have to be altered. Civil servants live and work in the city and pay no tax. Let L_c, G_c, and Y_c be the labour force, total real income, and total money income of civil servants. The rate of tax, t, imposed on all other social classes, is chosen to provide civil servants with a real income equal to the real net income of other workers. Some variables must be defined net or gross of tax. Subscripts n and g are added where relevant; for instance, the net and gross real income per worker in tons of grain are C_n and C_g, where

$$C_n = C_g(1-t). \tag{1'}$$

It is useful to define a net and gross transport cost in tons of grain per ton kilometre, the former, T_n, representing the actual deduction of grain by transport workers and the latter, T_g, representing the cost to someone employing a transport worker. Definitions of T_n and T_g are

$$T_g = C_g\beta \tag{2'}$$

and

$$T_n = C_n\beta = G_g\beta(1-t) = T_g(1-t). \tag{3'}$$

The estimation of the number of transport workers requires a new formula to account for taxation, but the method of deriving the formula is similar to the one used already. The output of grain from a ring is again

$$2\pi DO\varDelta D.$$

The proportion transported to the city is now

$$(1-\alpha+\alpha t),$$

which is the landlords' share of the grain plus the tax levied on the farm workers' share. The proportion of this grain arriving at the city depends not on the cost of transport but on that cost net of the tax paid by the transport worker, that is on T_n rather than on T_g. The amount of grain arriving in the city is therefore

$$2\pi DO(1-\alpha+\alpha t)e^{-T_n D}\varDelta D$$

and the number of transport workers required is equal to the amount of grain sent to the city, less the amount arriving, all divided by the consumption of grain per worker, that is

$$L_T = \int_0^{D*} 2\pi D(1-\alpha+\alpha t)\ (1-e^{-T_n D})\ \frac{1}{C_n}\ OdD. \qquad (4')$$

The rest of the variables can be estimated as before, with only minor and obvious changes in the formulae; an exception is Y_T, which is not relevant to the problem discussed in this appendix. Characteristics of these economies are easily computed by adding the primed formulae in this appendix to the equations in the main body of the chapter. The enlarged system of equations is solved and the results are presented as Table 7.

TABLE 7

The Contrast between an Economy where Civil Servants are required and an Economy where they are not

	A Civil servants required	B Civil servants not required
the rate of tax $t\%$	53·6	0·0
% farm workers L_F/L in the labour force	24·2	60·9
% transport workers L_T/L	43·1	39·1
% civil servants L_C/L	32·7	0·0
output of grain (million tons) G	2963	4703
net real income per worker (tons per year) C_n	2·46	3·34
net real income per landlord (tons per year) $\frac{Y_{sn}}{P(o)S}$	2·46	14·20
transport cost: kilos of grain per ton kilometre T or T_g	2·65	1·67

The interesting feature of the table is the contrast in the distribution of real income. Suppose economy B were being converted into economy A. All social classes would presumably gain from the activities of the civil servants, but they would lose different shares of their grain. The grain consumption of workers would be reduced by less than a third from 3·34 to 2·46 tons per head, but the grain consumption of landlords would be reduced by five-sixths, from 14·2 to 2·46 tons per head. Landlords lose both from the reduction in the total output of grain and from the increase in gross transport cost caused by the rise in the gross (pre-tax) wage rate in grain from 3·34 to 5·30 tons per year. The model seems to bear curious implications about the justice of the income tax. The activity of the civil servants may be absolutely necessary for the functioning of society or it may be optional in that benefits conferred on the community could be dispensed with without endangering the rest of economic life. Police protection is a necessary service, while the building and maintenance of public parks is optional. If the services of civil servants were necessary (in this sense), economy B could never be observed. But if the services of the civil servants were optional public goods, a society might find itself in the position of contemplating a change from situation A to situation B or vice versa. And if the distribution of income in the initial situation, whichever it is, is considered just, then the distribution of income in the new system is unjust. Consequently either the income tax is not a just tax, or taxes and subsidies should be imposed in the absence of any public expenditure.

The final row of the table reveals transport cost in kilos of grain per ton kilometre to be greater with public expenditure than without it. Consequently the decision to engage in public expenditure influences measurement of productivity by industry. Though real wages in both industries are the same, the ratio of the productivity of labour in agriculture to the productivity of labour in transport is lower in economy A than in economy B.

Appendix II

Placing manufactures into the model

There are many possible ways of adding a second commodity. The model as modified in this appendix takes on characteristics both of the model in the body of this chapter and of the model of Chapter 9.

The assumptions of the model in the body of this chapter are altered as follows

(1) There are three industries, agriculture, transport, and manufacturing. The agricultural production function is unchanged. The product of manufacturing is machines, the input is labour, and the production function is

$$M = \delta L_M \qquad (1'')$$

where M is the number of machines produced, L_M is the labour force in manufacturing, and δ is a technical parameter. It may be supposed that the raw material of manufactures is a free good. Manufacturing is restricted to the city.

(2) It requires β_G man-years of labour to carry one ton of grain one unit of distance, and β_M man-years of labour to carry one machine one unit of distance.

(3) It is no longer necessary to suppose that landlords live in the city because trade in machines and grain is sufficient to create demand for the services of transport workers. Landlords are now assumed to reside on their farms.

(4) Everyone consumes grain and manufactures in the same invariant proportion, namely γ machines per ton of grain. A more realistic theory of demand could be included in the model by letting γ be a function of real income per head and the relative price of grain and machines. We shall not do so.

(5) All workers are equally proficient at farming, manufacturing, and transport and there is free mobility of labour among these trades. This implies that real wages are the same everywhere, and in all occupations.

Suppose that, in equilibrium, the real wage is sufficient to buy C tons of grain and γC machines. The money wage $W(D)$ at each location must then be

$$W(D) = C(P_G(D) + \gamma P_M(D)) \qquad (2'')$$

where $P_G(D)$ and $P_M(D)$ are the prices of grain and machines at D. It follows from the assumption (2), concerning transport cost, that the change in each price with respect to distance is the product of the wage rate and the amount of labour in transport used or saved in moving one unit of distance away from the city:

$$\frac{\mathrm{d}}{\mathrm{d}D}\left\{P_G(D)\right\} = -\beta_G W(D), \qquad (3'')$$

and

$$\frac{\mathrm{d}}{\mathrm{d}D}\left\{P_M(D)\right\} = \beta_M W(D). \qquad (4'')$$

Equations $(2'')$, $(3'')$, and $(4'')$ jointly imply that

$$W(D) = W(0)e^{TD}, \qquad (5a'')$$

$$P_G(D) = P_G(0) - \beta_G W(0)\left(\frac{e^{TD} - 1}{T}\right), \qquad (6a'')$$

$$P_M(D) = P_M(0) + \beta_M W(0)\left(\frac{e^{TD} - 1}{T}\right), \qquad (7a'')$$

where

$$T = C(-\beta_G + \gamma\beta_M) \qquad (8'')$$

is the net change in the cost in man-years of labour of the normal bundle of goods consumed per worker as one moves away from the city. These equations show that as one moves away from the city, grain becomes cheaper, machines become more expensive, and the price level could become higher or lower depending on the sign of T, that is, on the ratio of the transport costs of grain and machines and on the proportion between grain and machines consumed.

If T takes the value zero, equations (5a), (6a), and (7a) must be replaced by

$$W(D) = W(0) \text{ (a constant)}, \qquad (5b'')$$
$$P_G(D) = P_G(0) - \beta_G D W(0), \qquad (6b'')$$
$$P_M(D) = P_M(0) - \beta_M D W(0). \qquad (7b'')$$

Note that there is always some D at which the price of grain falls to zero; this is the limit of cultivation. In the previous models all the available land was cultivated. In this model some land remains uncultivated if the price of grain falls to zero at a value of D less than D^*.

9

At each location D, the marginal product of a farm worker equals the real wage in grain

$$\alpha El(D)^{\alpha-1} = \frac{W(D)}{P_G(D)} \tag{8a''}$$

so that

$$l(D) = \left(\frac{\alpha EP_G(D)}{W(D)}\right)^{\frac{1}{1-\alpha}}. \tag{8b''}$$

The density of the farm labour force decreases steadily as one moves away from the city, because $P_G(D)$ becomes a continually smaller proportion of $W(D)$. This is in contrast to the property of the model in the body of this chapter that l, the density of the farm labour force, is the same everywhere. Farm labourers tend to cluster near the city to take advantage of the lower relative price of machines. The density, $l(D)$, at each location D is established so that the advantage to a man living near the city from the low price of machines, just compensates for the low marginal product of labour in agriculture caused by the greater concentration of the farm labour force.

The total output of grain, G, is

$$G = \int_0^D 2\pi DEl(D)^\alpha dD. \tag{9''}$$

Since both landlords and farm workers live on the farms, the amount of grain dispatched from each ring of width ΔD is $Z_G(D)\Delta D$, the output of grain multiplied by the proportion of the budget spent on machines,

$$Z_G(D) = 2\pi DEl(D)^\alpha \frac{\gamma P_M(D)}{P_G(D)+\gamma P_M(D)}. \tag{10''}$$

Equation (10'') shows the share of grain production dispatched to the city increasing with D, but this result is very much a consequence of the assumption that grain and machines are consumed in fixed proportions. Had γ not been assumed constant, had it, instead, been allowed to vary with prices, the share of grain production dispatched to the city would increase or decrease with D depending on whether

$$\gamma\{P_M(D) \div P_G(D)\}$$

increases or decreases, i.e. whether the price elasticity of demand for manufactures is greater or less than unity.

The rest of the equations in the system are easily derived. The consumption of grain by landlords, farm workers, and manufacturing workers are as follows:

$$G_S = (1-\alpha)\left\{G - \int_0^{D^*} Z_G(D)\mathrm{d}D\right\}, \tag{11''}$$

$$G_F = \frac{\alpha}{(1-\alpha)}G_S, \tag{12''}$$

$$G_M = CL_M. \tag{13''}$$

The consumption of grain by transport workers is

$$G_T = G - G_F - G_S - G_M. \tag{14''}$$

The consumption of machines by classes is

$$M_F = \gamma G_F, \tag{15''}$$
$$M_S = \gamma G_S, \tag{16''}$$
$$M_T = \gamma G_T, \tag{17''}$$
$$\text{and } M_M = \gamma G_M. \tag{18''}$$

The composition of the labour force is

$$L_F = \int_0^{D^*} 2\pi D l(D)\mathrm{d}D, \tag{19''}$$

$$L_T = \frac{G_T}{C}. \tag{20''}$$

The system is completed by the accounting identities

$$M = M_F + M_M + M_T + M_S \tag{21''}$$
and
$$L = L_F + L_M + L_T \tag{22''}$$

and equation determining the price of manufactures in the city,

$$\delta P_M(o) = C\{P_M(o) + \gamma P_G(o)\}. \tag{23''}$$

The meaning of this last equation is that the value of the output of one worker in manufacturing must equal the cost of the usual pattern of consumption in the city. The price of grain in the city, $P(o)$, is again a parameter. This system of equations is sufficient to determine L_F, L_M, L_T, G, G_F, G_M, G_T, G_S, M, M_F, M_M, M_T, M_S and the functions, $l(D)$, $P_M(D)$, $P_G(D)$, and $W(D)$ from given values of the parameters L, D^*, E, $P_G(o)$, α, β_G, β_M, δ, and γ.

The relation between real incomes and money incomes among social classes depends on the sign of T. If T is negative, the money wage rate declines continuously with distance from the city, and manufacturing workers appear most productive, transport workers next, and farm workers least, when all workers are in fact equally well off. If T is positive, the relation among apparent productivities is reversed. If $T = O$, all workers with the same real income appear equally productive, for in this case money income reflects real income as in an economy located at a single point in space.

11

Trade Taxes

TRADE taxes differ from other links in the chain of prices in that they originate outside the economy and may be imposed, removed, or altered at the decree of the public authority. This discretionary origin of the trade taxes makes their influence on income particularly disturbing, for it is a minimum requirement of an acceptable definition of income that income and its composition at any time be a fact upon which public policy may be grounded and not a variable that may be changed instantly at will.

The effects of trade taxes, taxes and subsidies on imports and exports, may be classified under three headings. First, trade taxes can increase or decrease the size of the national income in $U.S. to any desired extent; there is virtually no limit to how large or small the national income can be made to appear. Second, trade taxes can alter the composition of national income or the measured productivities of industries without altering the composition of the labour force or amounts of goods and services produced. Third, changes in domestic relative prices induced by trade taxes normally cause real changes in the composition of output, trade, and consumption. This last, and most important, effect is the subject of the greater part of the theory of international trade and we have nothing new to say about it. We are concerned with the first two effects and shall deal with them consecutively.

(a) TRADE TAXES AND THE SIZE OF THE NATIONAL INCOME IN $U.S. PER HEAD

A suitable combination of a tax on imports and a subsidy on exports can increase the national income in $U.S. to any desired extent. We begin with this mix of taxes because its effect on income is particularly easy to trace; this mix of taxes increases income without affecting domestic relative prices, output, or consumption.

Imagine a small country, small in the sense that a firm in perfect competition is small, facing perfectly elastic supply curves for its imports and perfectly elastic demand curves for its exports. The international currency is U.S. dollars. The country may buy or sell any amount of the traded commodities at world prices that are invariant in U.S. dollars. The exchange rate between this country's currency and U.S. dollars is allowed to fluctuate so that trade is balanced at all times. The foreign exchange rate is designated as F. The national income of this country is Y in units of its own currency, and is $Y^{\$}$ in U.S. dollars. In equilibrium,

$$Y^{\$} = \frac{Y}{F}. \tag{1}$$

It is convenient, though not absolutely necessary to the argument, to assume the truth of the crude quantity theory of money; we suppose that the money supply is fixed, and therefore Y, the national income at local prices, is constant.

The national income in \$U.S. can be increased by t per cent by the imposition of a tax on imports and subsidy on exports both levied at t per cent of world prices. World prices in dollars and domestic prices in the local currency are related by the formulae

$$\frac{P_I}{F} = P_I^{\$}\left(1 + \frac{t}{100}\right), \tag{2}$$

$$\frac{P_E}{F} = P_E^{\$}\left(1 + \frac{t}{100}\right), \tag{3}$$

where P_I and P_E are domestic prices in local currency, and $P_I^{\$}$ and $P_E^{\$}$ are world prices in dollars of imports and exports respectively. The imposition of the tax and subsidy cannot affect world prices because these are invariant. Equations (2) and (3) show that the domestic relative price of exports and imports remains unchanged. The total tax revenue is not affected because the tax and subsidy balance off when trade is in equilibrium. Even domestic prices P_I and P_E remain unchanged, because the price level is held firm by the quantity of money. The only variable that can give way in response to the imposition of the tax and subsidy is the foreign exchange rate. The foreign exchange rate, F, decreases, causing the national income in \$U.S. ($Y^{\$} = Y/F$) to increase by t per cent. Similarly, a combination of a subsidy on imports and a tax on exports causes national income to decrease. This proposition is a variant of the well-known theorem in international trade that an export subsidy combined with an import duty is the equivalent of a devaluation.

Had we supposed that a world currency, like gold, was used domestically, the foreign exchange rate could not change in response to a tariff and export subsidy (or to the opposite combination, an export tax and import subsidy), but domestic prices would change instead. The foreign exchange rate, F, in equations 2 and 3 would be fixed at unity, and domestic prices P_I and P_E would rise by $t\%$. Domestic prices of goods and services that do not enter into international trade would rise proportionally to preserve the structure of relative prices within the country, for the economic mechanism that sets relative prices within a country is not aware of changes in foreign trade unless these changes alter the relative price of exports and imports, and the combinations of taxes and subsidies we are considering are exactly those that preserve the relative price of exports and imports. Since all relative prices within the country remain unchanged, and since relative prices alone determine the composition of output and consumption, these combinations of trade taxes can have no real effects upon the economy. The rise in all prices causes the inflow of enough gold to finance the extra volume (in money terms, but not in real terms) of business. Finally, since prices rise while real economic activity remains unchanged, the national income rises by $t\%$.[1]

---

[1] There is a symmetry in the monetary effects of trade taxes that is different from the symmetry in their real effects. As A. P. Lerner has shown in 'The Symmetry between Export Taxes and Import Taxes', *Economica*, 1932, any tax on foreign trade diminishes the volume of trade by raising the relative price of imports with respect to exports, and it makes no difference to its trade-inhibiting effect whether the tax is imposed on exports or on imports. The symmetries among the real effects of the trade taxes are (a) between the export tax and import tax that reduce the incentive to trade and (b) between the export subsidy and import subsidy that increase the incentive to trade. The symmetries among the monetary effects are (a) between the export tax and the import subsidy that reduce national income in \$U.S. and (b) between the export subsidy and import tax that increase national income in \$U.S. The analogy between symmetries must not be pushed too far. A uniform tariff on all imports causes a change in the national income in \$U.S. in the same direction but not necessarily of the same magnitude as the change caused by an equal rate of subsidy on exports.

Though the (positive or negative) export subsidy and import tax is the only combination of trade taxes that has no real effect on the economy, other combinations of trade taxes have predictable monetary effects. In general, the national income valued in the world currency is buoyed up by

(a) a subsidy on exports,

(b) a tax on the import of commodities that are substitutes for commodities made at home, and

(c) a subsidy on imported raw material, machinery, or other factors of production.

The truth of this statement is easily demonstrated if we suppose that the world currency is used domestically. This assumption makes no real difference to the analysis but it is convenient because it serves to keep the foreign exchange rate out of the equations: if $P_i^\$$ is the world price of the commodity i, and t_i is the rate of subsidy on the export or tax on the import of the commodity of i, then the domestic price is $P_i^\$(1+t_i/100)$. The world market may be thought of as confronting the economy of a country with a pattern of gaps between the prices of the outputs of all industries and the costs, per unit of output, of imported raw material and semi-finished products. For each commodity, i, the price gap per unit of output is

$$P_i^\$ - \sum_j a_{ij} P_j^\$, \tag{4}$$

where $P_i^\$$ and $P_j^\$$ are world prices of the commodity i and imported raw material or semi-finished product j, and a_{ij} is the requirement of j in the production of i. The gap as seen by domestic producers is

$$P_i^\$\left(1+\frac{t_i}{100}\right) - \sum_j a_{ij} P_j^\$\left(1+\frac{t_i}{100}\right), \tag{5}$$

where the t_i and t_j are rates of tariff or subsidy which may be positive or negative. The national income, a quantity-weighted sum of these price gaps, is buoyed up when any price gap is increased without other price gaps being decreased. It may be seen at once from formula 5 that an increase in t_i, a tax on imports or a subsidy on exports, increases the domestic price gap and raises national income accordingly, and that an increase in t_j, a tax on an imported raw material, decreases the price gap and decreases national income accordingly. The real effects of trade taxes magnify their monetary effects because resources flow from activities in which price gaps decrease to activities in which price gaps increase. Similarly, since untraded commodities tend on balance to be substitutes for traded commodities in production and in use, increases in national income caused by changes in domestic prices of traded commodities are magnified by induced increases in prices of commodities that do not enter into international trade.

A really perverse national income office that had sufficient influence on public policy to control the rates of trade taxes could play havoc with statistics of national income in $U.S. per head, making a poor country look absurdly rich or a rich country look absurdly poor. This does not happen because tariffs are imposed for other reasons. What does happen is that tariffs imposed to alter the real economic situation have side-effects on income measurement. For instance the rice-exporting countries of South-East Asia tend to have their incomes biased down because the export of rice is heavily taxed and because rice is a large part of total output and a close substitute in production and in use for many other agricultural commodities. By contrast, European countries that protect domestic industries by import duties, by subsidies on exports, and by allowing duty-free import of industrial raw materials, have larger money incomes than they would have if there were no trade taxes and public revenue were got by other means.

(b) TRADE TAXES AND THE MEASUREMENT OF PRODUCTIVITY

The price mechanism must influence any comparison of productivity by industry because there is no way of comparing contributions to welfare of bushels of grain and tons of steel other than by their prices. Productivity measures are inevitably affected by changes in world prices or in home demand. But since productivity statistics are data on which public policy is grounded, it might be hoped that productivity statistics would represent economic conditions prior to public policy, that productivity statistics would be invariant with respect to public policy except in the long run as public policy influences fundamental economic conditions in the composition of the labour force and in the physical volume of output.

This ideal is not attained when productivity by industry is measured as 'income per man employed' in the usual way, for this statistic can be affected by trade taxes even if these taxes have no effect on production or on the distribution of the labour force. Virtually any combination of productivities can be obtained by a suitable choice of trade taxes.

The effect of trade taxes on productivity is so similar to their effect on total income in $U.S. that both influences can be described by the same formula. Consider once again the expression in equation 5 for domestic value added per unit of output as a function of world prices and domestic trade taxes.

Since productivity is value added divided by the labour force, the productivity of an industry is increased by any tax or subsidy that increases value added in that industry. A country that raises revenue by taxing agricultural exports, at once decreases its national income in $U.S. and lowers measured productivity in agriculture. A country that protects home industries by a tariff increases its national income in $U.S. and makes the protected industries appear more productive.[1]

It is especially important to distinguish productivity as it would be without a tariff from productivity caused by the tariff, when productivity statistics are cited as evidence justifying a tariff. There is a proposition in international trade theory that a tariff may be beneficial by inducing factors of production to move from industries where their productivity is low to industries where their productivity is higher.[2] On the strength of this proposition, evidence of a marked disparity between the productivities of agriculture and manufacturing in underdeveloped countries has been cited as a justification for protection of manufactures. What may pass unnoticed is that manufacturing productivity is high because manufacturing is protected and the export of agricultural products is taxed. The imposition of a tariff automatically produces evidence for its justification. Of course the argument for tariffs may be

[1] To protect an industry or an activity is to increase its apparent productivity, and our formula for the price gaps is closely related to the measure of effective protection. See W. M. Corden, 'The Structure of a Tariff System and the Effective Rate', *Journal of Political Economy*, Vol. LXXIV (1966).

[2] The case for this proposition is presented by E. E. Hagen in 'An Economic Justification for Protectionism', *Quarterly Journal of Economics*, Vol. 72 (1958).

valid in a particular case; the relevant evidence is the comparison of productivity prior to the imposition of trade taxes.

This line of reasoning leads to the idea that the productivity statistics required for assessing benefits of tariffs or for comparing efficiency by industry or for contrasting ratios of productivities by industry among countries, is income per man employed as it would be if all public revenue were obtained by an income tax. The income tax is the preferred standard for productivity measurement because it allows domestic prices to differ from world prices by no more that the cost of trading and because it allows the market price of each good to reflect marginal utility and marginal factor cost. Statistics computed in this way would seem to provide the information one hopes to get from productivity measurements. There are some statistical difficulties in estimating income as it would be under a different tax system, but these do not concern us now, for they are discussed in Part III.

Difficulties of a more fundamental kind arise in the choice of the rate of progression of the tax. A high limit of exemption or steep rate of progression in a poor country would place the entire burden of the tax on to the urban sectors, inhibiting the growth of manufacturing, raising the value added per unit of manufactures relative to the value added per unit of agriculture, and causing labour in manufacturing to appear relatively productive. Similarly, as shown in Appendix I of Chapter 10, the essentially political decision to increase or decrease the scope of public services may well affect income per worker in different places and different trades. It is unlikely that these qualifications to the rule of thumb that the income tax is neutral for productivity measurement would make much difference to the final statistics, but, in strict logic, there is no neutral tax from which true productivity figures can be measured. Shadow productivities are in part a consequence of one's view of a just system of public revenue and expenditure.

PART III

THE INTERPRETATION OF THE NATIONAL INCOME OF THAILAND

Introduction

NATIONAL income statistics are a medium, perhaps the principle medium, through which we see an economy. Our study of prices and the national income may in retrospect be thought of as an investigation of whether the image seen through the medium is true or distorted, and of how we may apply corrections to a medium to set the image right.

The national income of Thailand is to be studied partly for its own sake and partly as an example of how the theory may be used in refining and interpreting national income statistics. Most of the ideas and concepts developed so far are to reappear in our study of Thailand, but we shall not allow the theory to restrict our choice of methods of analysis or to confine the range of our interests. Where theory was formerly dominant, it is now subordinate to the question: To what extent do the national income statistics of Thailand convey an accurate picture of the Thai economy?

The net national income, the industrial distribution of the gross domestic product, and the labour force of Thailand are shown in Tables 8 and 9. These tables reveal many features of the Thai economy, but two facts stand out above the rest. First, the net national income is 58 thousand million baht, equivalent to £34·59 per head when baht are converted to £ at the foreign exchange rate of 58 baht to the £; this should imply that the standard of living of most Thai is well below the level of subsistence. Second, the 81·5 per cent of the labour force employed in farming produces only 30·2 per cent of the national product; this should imply that the productivity of labour in agriculture is only a tenth of the productivity of labour in other industries.[1] Our object in Part III

[1] The ratio of the productivity of agriculture to the productivity of other sectors is $[30·2 \div 81·5] \div [(100-30·2) \div (100-81·5)]$. Agriculture is defined in this computation to include crops and livestock only.

is to examine these two 'facts' revealed by the national income statistics to see if they are really facts, or merely distortions caused by the medium through which we see the facts.

TABLE 8

The Gross Domestic Product of Thailand at Current Prices 1963

	Million baht	Per cent
Agriculture, total	23 722	35·1
rice	9041	13·4
other crops	9378	13·8
livestock	2007	3·0
fisheries	1705	2·5
forestry	1591	2·4
Manufacturing	7938	11·7
Mining and quarrying	1063	1·6
Construction	3892	5·7
Electricity and water supply	320	0·5
Transport and communication	5751	8·5
Wholesale and retail trade	12 081	17·9
Banking, insurance and real estate	1835	2·7
Ownership of dwellings	3482	5·1
Public administration and defence	3290	4·9
Services	4277	6·3
Total GDP	67 650	100
Net national income	57 862	

Source: National Income Statistics of Thailand, Office of the Prime
   Minister, Bangkok.

Chapters 13 and 15 are critical examinations of these facts. The revaluation in Chapter 13 of the Thai national income at British prices increases the income per head almost fivefold, from £34·55 to £162·47. Similarly the revaluation of the British national income at Thai prices decreases the income per head by about a half, from £450·97 to £217·10. Corrections in Chapter 15 to statistics of income per man employed, as indicators of productivity by industry, increase the ratio of agricultural to non-agricultural productivity from a tenth to about a third.

TABLE 9

The Industrial Distribution of the Thai Labour Force 1960[1] (thousand)

Occupation	No. male (1)	No. female (2)	No. male and female (3)	as % of labour force
Agriculture (including livestock)	5465	5721	11 186	81·5
Forestry, hunting, and fishing	111	37	148	1·1
Mining and quarrying	22	7	29	0·2
Manufacturing	294	177	471	3·4
Construction	62	6	68	0·4
Electricity, water supply	15	1	16	0·1
Commerce	363	417	780	5·7
Transport, storage and communications	156	9	165	1·2
Services	458	197	655	4·8
Other	159	93	252	1·8
Total	7107	6665	13 772	100

Source: Statistical Year Book Thailand 1964.

Rice provides a particularly good illustration of the chain of prices. Prices from the Thai farmer to the British consumer are presented in Chapter 14 as an explanation of the differential observed in Chapter 13, and as raw material for the computations in Chapter 15. As an important by-product, the chain of prices reveals the cost and to some extent efficiency of distribution in Thailand and in the U.K.

[1] In accordance with the practice of the Thai National Income Office the labour force in 1963 is estimated by adding 9 per cent to the 1960 Census figures. In 1963, the population of Thailand was 28,835 thousand and the population of the U.K. was 53,678 thousand.

13

Income as a Measure of Welfare: A Comparison of Real Income in Thailand and the United Kingdom

IMAGINE a foreign aid programme conducted by the U.K. in which the total resources available are divided among the recipient countries by a formula that takes economic welfare into account. Economic welfare in this context is defined by a conceptual experiment. In a comparison between Thailand and U.K., a typical Englishman is supposed to choose the sum of money in England that would leave him neither better nor worse off than he would be in Thailand earning the typical Thai income. This sum of money in pounds, Thai real income by British standards, is the measure of economic welfare in Thailand. In principle, tests of this kind could be conducted for many countries, so that economic welfare might be compared among them. This test is not one that a statistician would apply in practice. Instead it is a guide to the statistician in organizing his material. In this chapter, incomes of Thailand and the U.K. are compared with this criterion in mind, as if the results of the comparison were to be used in assessing the state of poverty or wealth of Thailand in the light of a foreign aid programme.

Most commodities are defined quite broadly and little account is taken of differences in quality. This is desirable in a comparison emphasizing the extent of poverty because quality differences and fine substitutions among technically similar commodities are more important for the rich than for the poor. Broadly defined commodities are often imposed upon the comparison by the nature of the available statistics. Vegatables for instance cannot be subdivided into lettuce, tomatoes, etc., because this item in the Thai accounts is based on a single guess of consumption per head. Legal, medical, educational, and religious services are measured by numbers of practitioners and there is no way of knowing whether the Thai lawyers, doctors, or teachers are objectively better or worse than their British counterparts. On the other hand, an undesirable allowance for quality differences enters the comparison when complete absence of quantity data or direct measurements of relative prices, compels us to suppose that prices of durable goods and financial services are the same in Thailand and the U.K.

Comparisons are prepared at British prices and at Thai prices. The comparison at British prices would seem to correspond more closely to the concept of income we have in mind but the comparison at Thai prices is relevant because it probably yields an over-estimate of the desired ratio of British to Thai incomes while the comparison at British prices yields an underestimate. Several methods are used to revalue the components of national income at common price weights. The preferred method, used for instance in comparing food consumption, is to break down values in both countries into prices and quantities. If only price or only quantity is available, the other may be estimated; price may be estimated by dividing value by quantity, and quantity may be estimated by dividing value by price. For instance, the quantity of 'personal care' is estimated by dividing its value by the relative price of huircuts. When values in the accounts cannot be completely identified with a set of comparable quantities, a single commodity may be treated as a surrogate for the whole class; for instance, yards of cloth is treated as a surrogate for clothing in general. When values cannot be broken down into prices and quantities, and when neither a surrogate for quantity nor a reasonable price index presents itself, recourse is had to one of two methods. Either the exchange rate is assumed to represent a proper purchasing power parity for that item or the ratio of real incomes associated with that item is set arbitrarily in accordance with what the author thinks reasonable. Durable goods, other than automobiles, are dealt with by the first method and housing is dealt with by the second.

The methods of comparison shade imperceptibly one into the other, and the arbitrariness, obviously present in the last method, is nowhere absent altogether. As shown in Part I, it enters in a fundamental way in the choice of commodities and in the decision that such and such items in Thailand and the U.K. represent equal amounts of the same commodity. From a logical point of view, there is not much difference between saying that a kilo of Thai fruit equals a kilo of British fruit, and saying that a unit of Thai accommodation equals half a unit of British accommodation, though as a matter of practice, we are less disturbed by the former judgement than by the latter. Comparison of national incomes can organize our judgements about the different commodities and draw out of our judgements their joint implication about comparative living standards. But it cannot dispense with the need for judgement, and it can never be wholly free of subjectivity.

The scope of income is fairly conventional. Defence is excluded because suitable Thai data are lacking, and there are no adjustments to income for expenditure of foreigners inside the country or for the balance of payments. Otherwise the definition of income is much the same as that in the British or Thai accounts. Some variations in the income concept are examined briefly at the end of the chapter. As a rule, the values of the Thai income at Thai prices and British income at British prices are the same as in the official accounts, but occasionally, for instance in valuing legal and religious services, it has been thought best to depart slightly from the values in the official accounts. Thai and British incomes total to £451 and £36 per head in this computation as against £451 and £34·6 in the official accounts. The comparison is, of course, of the expenditure side of the national accounts. The date chosen is 1963.

For convenience, all Thai prices and values are stated in pounds, or decimal fractions of pounds, converted from the Thai currency at the foreign exchange rate of 58 baht to the pound. Instead of saying that an automobile in Thailand costs 30 000 baht, we would say that it costs £517·24 (30·000÷58). Thus even though Thailand and the U.K. have different currencies, we may speak unambiguously of the ratios of the Thai and British price levels for classes of goods and for national income as a whole.

The main comparison is presented as Table 10. The first column is the Thai income per head per annum converted into British pounds by the foreign exchange rate. For instance the item £13·62 for food is

$$\frac{\text{value of food consumption in baht}}{\text{(the exchange rate between baht and £)} \times \text{(population of Thailand}}$$

The second column is the U.K. income per head per annum. The third column is the income of the U.K. when all the U.K. commodities are valued at Thai prices in pounds (i.e. Thai prices divided by the foreign exchange rate). The fourth column is the Thai income when Thai quantities are valued at British prices. The fifth column is the ratio of British and Thai incomes when all prices are converted to pounds by the foreign exchange rate. The sixth column is the geometric average of the ratios of the U.K. income and the Thai income at Thai prices and at British prices, i.e.

$$\sqrt{\left(\frac{\sum P_U Q_U}{\sum P_U Q_T} \cdot \frac{\sum P_T Q_U}{\sum P_T Q_T}\right)}.$$

The seventh column is the ratio of the fifth and sixth. This is the implicit ratio of U.K. to Thai prices when all prices are converted into pounds. For instance, the figure of 3·27 in the second row means that British food prices are as the whole 327 per cent of Thai food prices. A detailed description of the sources of data in Table 10 is presented as an appendix to this chapter.

The most interesting feature of the table is the contrast between the comparison of incomes in money terms and the comparison at U.K. prices. The comparison in money terms shows the U.K. income per head to be 13·05 times the Thai income per head, the comparison at Thai prices shows the U.K. income per head to be 6·28 times the Thai income per head, and the comparison at U.K. prices shows the U.K. income per head to be only 2·78 times the Thai income per head. This last figure, though something of an underestimate of the relative prosperity of the U.K., probably comes the nearest of the three figures to the ratio required by our test of economic welfare. The human meaning of these figures can perhaps best be appreciated by considering the income, inclusive of public administration and capital formation, of a family of four people. The gross income of a family in the U.K. is £1792 (448 × 4). The apparent gross income of a Thai family is only £138 per annum, but the value at U.K. prices of the purchases of a Thai family of four people is £650. This is what it would cost to buy the Thai bundle of goods in Britain. Allowing for the redistributive effect of the system of tax and public expenditure in the U.K., and for substitutions from the Thai pattern of consumption, we might reduce this figure to—say—£550. It is with a British worker who supports a family of four and who pays some of the

TABLE 10

National Income Per Head in Thai and and the U.K. 1963

(All values in £ per head per annum)

	(1) $P_T Q_T$	(2) $P_U Q_U$	(3) $P_T Q_U$	(4) $P_U Q_T$	(5) $\dfrac{P_U Q_U}{P_T Q_T}$	(6) Geometric average of comparisons at Thai and U.K. prices	(7) The ratio of the U.K. price to the Thai price: column 5 divided by column 6
Consumption	28·37	375·49	165·22	144·60	13·23	3·89	3·40
(a) food	13·62	99·39	37·57	55·24	7·30	2·23	3·27
(b) alcohol, tobacco and soft drinks	1·89	49·11	29·47	22·44	25·98	6·71	3·87
(c) clothing	2·07	31·93	7·32	9·02	15·42	3·54	4·36
(d) housing (rent and fuel)	2·92	54·70	5·84	27·35	18·73	2 assumed	9·37
(e) purchases transport and communication	3·07	17·05	10·43	6·66	4·50	2·45	1·84

(f) automobiles	0·52	23·59	24·52	0·53	45·33	45·63	0·99
(g) other durables	0·65	22·37	22·37	0·65	34·41	34·41	1 assumed
(h) personal care and misc. household expenditure	0·72	14·68	4·89	2·16	20·38	6·79	3 assumed
(i) domestic service	0·10	1·60	0·22	0·75	15·39	2·12	7·26
(j) recreation	0·92	19·00	6·33	2·76	20·65	6·88	3 assumed
(k) health	1·11	16·22	6·87	2·14	14·61	6·85	2·13
(l) education	0·75	16·52	1·28	9·71	22·02	1·70	12·95
(m) finance and expenditure abroad	0·14	10·54	10·54	0·14	75·29	75·29	1 assumed
(n) legal religious services	0·15	1·97	0·11	5·42	13·13	0·52	25·25
Public administration	1·52	25·56	2·96	13·10	16·82	1·95	8·63
Net capital formation	4·40	46·74	46·74	4·40	10·62	10·62	1 assumed
Total	34·55	450·97	217·10	162·47	13·05	4·18	3·12

$$\frac{\Sigma P_{iU} Q_{iU}}{\Sigma P_{iU} Q_{iT}} = 2.78; \qquad \frac{\Sigma P_{iT} Q_{iU}}{\Sigma P_{iT} Q_{iT}} = 6.28.$$

cost of public administration and investment on £550 a year in 1963, that an average Thai may be compared. This man is poor but he is not impossibly poor as the statistics in Table 1 would lead one to believe.

There is a risk in making comparisons among components of income of one's assumptions and judgements in constructing the statistics reappearing as inferences from the evidence. Six out of the sixteen rows, exclusive of totals, in Table 10 have arbitrary assignments in column 6 or 7 and the remainder of the items are arbitrary to some extent. The evidence in column 7 that durable goods are relatively more expensive in Thailand than food is no stronger than the assumption that the price of durable goods is the same in both countries. With this warning in mind, a few interesting observations can be made.

The proposition discussed in Chapter 8 Part II that the comparison of incomes through the foreign exchange rate undervalues the income from untraded products in poor countries is strikingly illustrated in Table 10. All of the very large price differentials, say those over fivefold, pertain to untradeable products—domestic service, education, legal and religious services, public administration, and housing.

The hypothesis in Chapter 9 that asymmetrical transport cost may bias income comparison also comes off well, but partly for the wrong reasons. According to the table, the foreign exchange rate establishes an approximate purchasing power parity in the imports of Thailand, but not in exports, and the form of the asymmetry biases the Thai income down. But this result might be due to my unwillingness to set any price level of column 7 at less than unity. It is of course possible for all prices of final goods and service to be lower in one country than in another. Imports might be exclusively of intermediate products, or the relative poverty of a country might force down the value added in distribution. I think there is a tendency in this direction in Thailand, but Table 10 furnishes no evidence because this hypothesis entered into its construction.

Rates of investment are particularly sensitive to the choice of price weights. When the incomes of Thailand and the U.K. are valued at local relative prices, the Thai rate of investment is a fifth higher than the U.K. rate. But the U.K. rate of investment appears markedly higher than the Thai rate of investment when incomes are revalued at either set of prices.

The rough equality between Thai and British investment rates at local prices is also altered by redefining net investment to be the excess over and above the investment needed to preserve intact the capital stock per head. Over the last fifteen years, the rates of population growth in Thailand and the United Kingdom have been 3% and 0·6%. Suppose that, in both countries, the return

TABLE 11

The Ratios of Investment to Income

	of Thailand	of the U.K.
at Thai prices	12·7%	21·5%
at U.K. prices	2·7%	10·4%

to non-human factors of production is ⅓ of income and the rate of interest is 10%. Capital-output ratios are then equal to 10/3, and rates of capital formation net of requirements to preserve the capital stock per head are the numbers in Table 11 reduced by 10 per cent (3⅓ × 3 per cent) in Thailand and by 2 per cent (3⅓ × 0·6) in the United Kingdom. Rates of net capital formation at local prices become 2·7 per cent in Thailand and 8·4 per cent in the United Kingdom. When rates of investment are computed in the usual way, Thailand appears to have the higher rate of investment, and in some sense this implication of the statistics is correct. But the United Kingdom has the greater rate of investment when both incomes are valued at a common set of prices, and when the preservation of capital per head is the basis for assessing the magnitude of net income and net investment.

The main finding of Table 10, that the real national income of Thailand is a very much larger proportion of the real national income of the U.K. than is implied by the conversion of both incomes into a common currency unit by the foreign exchange rate, can be restated in terms of price differentials. Table 10 shows the Thai price level to be about a third of that in the U.K. The one survey that compares Thai and British prices directly has come up with a very different result. The United Nations has recorded price levels in the capital cities of many countries as a basis for setting cost of living allowance for its personnel.[1] The index is set at 100 for New York city, and price levels of other cities are recorded as percentages above or below New York. In 1958 London was 85 and Bangkok was 123. Thai prices appear 45 per cent higher than British prices instead of 65 per cent lower as indicated in Table 10.[2]

The occurrence of this discrepancy illustrates the importance of knowing whose welfare is at issue in an income comparison. Table 10 is a comparison for an average man, with quality differences deliberately under-emphasized. The U.N. index is a comparison for rich men, for U.N. officials enjoy a standard of living well above average living standards in Thailand or the United Kingdom; the price index is weighted toward luxury items and toward items that must be imported into Thailand, and it takes account of the best quality of every good and service. This is what is required of a price index for U.N. personnel. The cost of living in Thailand is high for the rich and low for the poor.

Finally there is the question of why the price differentials are so large. It is not surprising to find large differentials in services like law, public administration, and medicine, that cannot enter into international trade. But it is odd to encounter a price differential of, for instance, 359 per cent in cereals when the major Thai cereal, rice, is a relatively imperishable commodity that enters in a large way in international trade. It is to this question that we turn in the next chapter. Our scope will be limited to the study of a single commodity, rice, but we shall trace its price through many stages of trade in an attempt to explain the total differential in terms of the forces set out in the 'chain of prices' in Table 6 of Chapter 6.

[1] *Retail Price Comparison for International Salary Determination*, Statistical Papers, series M, no. 14, Addendum 2.

[2] Between 1957 and 1963, the Thai cost of living index rose from 142 to 143 (*Statistical Yearbook, Thailand 1964*, Table 179), while the British retail price index rose from 109 to 120 (*Annual Abstract of Statistics 1965*, Table 373). If these indices are comparable with each other and with the U.N. index, then the differential in living costs has been reduced from 45 to 36 per cent.

Appendix

Computations in preparing Table 10

The main published sources of the data in the comparison are *National Income Statistics of Thailand, 1964 Edition; Statistical Yearbook, Thailand* 1964; *National Income and Expenditure 1964* (H.M.S.O., London); and *Annual Abstract of Statistics* 1965 (H.M.S.O., London). These will be abbreviated as *N.I.T.*, *S.Y.T.*, *N.I.E.*, and *A.A.S.* respectively. In addition, extensive use is made of unpublished material from the files of the National Income Office of Thailand.

(a) FOOD

Quantities of food consumed in Thailand and in the U.K. are estimated from food supplies. The British data on quantities are from *A.A.S.*, Table 218, 'Food supplies per head of population', (p. 182). The Thai data were furnished by the Thai National Income Office. Consumption of rice, the only cereal recorded in the accounts, is estimated from an expenditure survey. Consumption of all other commodities is estimated from production figures with adjustments for foreign trade. However, the production figures of vegetables and fruit are themselves guesses based on assumptions about 'reasonable' consumption levels.

Thai prices were furnished by the National Income Office. British prices were taken from Appendix B, Tables 1 and 2 of *Domestic Food Consumption and Expenditure: 1963* (Ministry of Agriculture, Fisheries and Food, H.M.S.O.). Unit values in each category of food were computed by dividing expenditure by quantity consumed.

In the comparison of food consumption in Table 12, quantities are in pounds (lb) per head per annum, and prices are in shillings

TABLE 12 *Food*
(prices are in shillings per lb. and quantities are lbs. per head per annum)

| | Thailand | | U.K. | | | | | |
	P_T	Q_T	P_U	Q_U	P_TQ_T	P_UQ_U	P_TQ_U	P_UQ_T
milk and cheese	0·34	18·9	0·82	410·1	6·43	336·28	136·43	15·49
meat	1·29	19·3	3·84	155·9	24·88	598·66	201·11	74·11
fish	1·15	56·7	3·84	19·3	62·20	74·11	22·20	217·73
eggs	1·57	5·8	2·69	33·5	9·11	90·12	52·60	15·60
fats	1·58	1·4	2·65	58·1	2·21	153·97	91·80	3·71
sugar	0·76	13·6	0·89	112·6	10·34	100·21	85·58	12·10
vegetables	0·16	62·7	0·93	126·5	10·03	117·65	20·24	58·31
fruit	0·16	220·4	1·37	96·6	35·26	132·34	15·46	301·95
coffee, tea, cocoa	3·27	0·4	6·77	13·7	1·31	92·75	44·80	2·71
spices	0·67	11·5	3·00	—	7·71	—	—	34·50
cereals	0·32	320·5	1·15	253·7	102·56	291·76	81·18	368·58
		Total: shillings per head			272·32	1987·82	751·39	1104·80
		Total: £ per head			13·62	99·39	37·57	55·24

$$\frac{\Sigma P_{iU}Q_{iU}}{\Sigma P_{iT}Q_{iT}} = 7·30 \qquad \frac{\Sigma P_{iU}Q_{iU}}{\Sigma P_{iU}Q_{iU}} = 1·80 \qquad \frac{\Sigma P_{iT}Q_{iU}}{\Sigma P_{iT}Q_{iT}} = 2·76$$

Fisher index = 2·23

per pound with Thai prices converted to pounds at the foreign exchange rate. Potatoes classed in the British statistics as a vegetable are included under the heading of cereals, because potatoes are more nearly substitutes for bread and rice than for other vegetables. Three pounds of potatoes are treated as equivalent to one pound of milled wheat or rice, in accordance with the calorific equivalence. The premium in the price of rice over the price of wheat in virtually all the world markets is not taken into account in setting quantity units of cereals; a pound of rice is treated as equivalent to a pound of wheat flour or of bread. All milk products are converted into pints of milk which are then converted into pounds. Condensed milk is converted into fresh milk at a ratio of four to one by weight. Cheese is converted into milk at British relative prices. No cheese enters into the Thai accounts, though a small amount of cheese is imported for the foreign community. Thai spices are valued in the U.K. at three shillings a pound; at this price, the value of U.K. consumption of spices is very small.

No allowance is made for quality differences in food, for food preparation, or for services of restaurants. The only Thai data on value added of restaurants is from tax receipts, and there is no way of allocating this data into prices and quantities. Casual observation leads me to believe that there are at least as many restaurants in Thailand as in the United Kingdom. I have no way of comparing qualities of food.

(b) ALCOHOL, TOBACCO AND SOFT DRINKS

British quantities consumed are from Tables 203, 216, 272, and 273 of *A.A.S.*; consumption of spirits is estimated as production plus imports less exports. British prices are estimated by dividing these quantities into the values in the national accounts in Table 18, 'Consumers' expenditure at current prices, Alcoholic drink and tobacco', *N.I.E.* (p. 19). Thai prices and quantities were furnished by the National Income Office. Quantities are from estimates of production, and prices are wholesale prices with an assumed retail mark-up. The British statistics express amounts of spirits in proof gallons while the Thai statistics express amounts in litres. The statistics are reconciled by supposing that Thai spirits are 70 per cent proof. Quantities of soft drinks are recorded in the U.K. statistics as 'gallons' produced, and in the Thai

TABLE 13

Alcohol, Tobacco and Soft Drinks

(All values and prices are in £ and all quantities are per head per annum)

	Thailand		U.K.		$P_T Q_T$	$P_U Q_U$	$P_T Q_U$	$P_U Q_T$
	Q_T	P_T	Q_U	P_U				
beer (litres)	0·318	0·277	88·414	0·146	0·09	12·91	24·49	0·05
spirit (litres)	3·225	0·203	8·106	1·119	0·66	9·07	1·65	3·61
tobacco (pounds)	3·666	0·242	4·769	5·023	0·89	23·96	1·15	18·41
soft drinks (litres)	3·336	0·076	28·820	0·110	0·25	3·17	2·18	0·37
Total					1·89	49·11	29·47	22·44

$$\frac{\Sigma P_{iU} Q_{iU}}{\Sigma P_{iT} Q_{iT}} = 25\cdot98 \qquad \frac{\Sigma P_{iU} Q_{iU}}{\Sigma P_{iU} Q_{iT}} = 2\cdot89 \qquad \frac{\Sigma P_{iT} Q_{iU}}{\Sigma P_{iT} Q_{iT}} = 15\cdot59 \qquad \text{Fisher index} = 6\cdot71$$

statistics as 'bottles' costing one baht each. It is assumed in constructing table 13 that the U.K. price of soft drinks is six pence per eight ounces, and that the size of each bottle in Thailand is eight ounces.

(a) CLOTHING

There is no satisfactory way of comparing amounts of clothing. Complete statistics are not available, and it is not clear what would be done with statistics if they were, for different sorts of clothing are worn in temperate and tropical countries. The values of clothing in the first and second columns of Table 10 are taken directly from the national accounts (*N.I.E.*, Table 18, 'Clothing'; and *N.I.T.*, Table 20, 4). Figures in the other columns under the heading of clothing are estimated by treating yards of cloth in apparel as a surrogate for clothing of all kinds. The amount of cloth consumed in the United Kingdom is estimated as the combined production of cotton goods, wool cloth, and cloth of man-made fibres (*A.A.S.*, Table 180), reduced by the difference between exports (*A.A.S.*, Table 273) and imports (*A.A.S.*, Table 272), and by the proportion (37 per cent) of cotton, wool, and man-made fibres receiving their final use, not as apparel, but as household goods or industrial fibre ('Approximate consumption of fibres by final uses in the United Kingdom and the E.E.C.', Table 11, Appendix VII, *Industrial Fibres*, Commonwealth Economic Committee, 1965). Though a small amount of silk cloth is used, cotton is by far the most widely-used material in Thailand, and only cotton is taken into account in the estimate of Thai consumption of cloth. An estimate of cotton textile production is take from *Bank of Thailand Monthly Report*, July 1965 (Table V.9). This figure is increased by 50 per cent to account for imports of cotton cloth and clothing. There is no adjustment for cloth not used in apparel because the proportion is unknown and probably quite small.

According to these calculations, the British consume twenty-six yards of cloth per head per annum in apparel, and the Thai consume seven yards per head per annum in apparel. The ratio of these numbers, actually $25 \cdot 78/7 \cdot 20$, serves as an index of consumption for transforming $P_U Q_U$ and $P_T Q_T$ into $P_U Q_T$ and $P_T Q_U$ in Table 10.

(d) HOUSING: RENT, FUEL, AND LIGHTING

To subsume rent, fuel, and lighting under the general heading of housing is to treat these items as joint products in consumption. Values are from the national accounts (*N.I.E.*, Table 18, 'Housing' and 'Fuel and Light'; and *N.I.T.*, Table 20, 'Rents, rates, and water charges' and 'Fuel and light'). I cannot think of any satisfactory way of constructing an index of real housing services in Thailand and the United Kingdom, and am reduced to assuming that the standard of housing in Thailand is equivalent to what could be obtained in the U.K. for half of the average expenditure on housing in the U.K. In 1963 the average British family (3·02 people) renting unfurnished accommodation spent 31·5 shillings a week on rent and 25·3 shillings on fuel, light, and power (Table I, *Family Expenditure Survey, Report for* 1963, H.M.S.O.). I judge that the typical house of a Thai farmer is as comfortable as the accommodation that could be got in Britain for 15 shillings a week, plus 13 shillings expenditure on fuel, light, and power.

(e) PURCHASED TRANSPORT AND COMMUNICATION

Quantities in Table 14 are from *A.A.S.*, Tables 232, 241, and 262 and from *S.Y.T.*, Tables 122, 115, 137–139, and 143; however, the number of public road vehicles in Thailand includes 10·9 thousand motor boats, as estimated by the Thai National Income Office. The estimate of the number of passenger-kilometres travelled on railroads in the U.K. is based on statistics of the British Railways and the London Transport Railways. One telegram is counted as ten telephone calls. Letters in Thailand and the United Kingdom are priced at a rate of threepence each. All other prices are imputed. The Thai National Income Office estimated the values of the services of railroads, telephones, and telegraphs from the revenues of public companies, and it estimated values of bus services from informed guesses about the income accruing to the different types of vehicles. Values of the services of buses, telephones, and telegraphs in the U.K. are from the national accounts ('Travel: other' and 'Communication services: telephone and telegraph', Table 18, *N.I.E.*) and the value of the services of railways is measured by the revenue of the passenger services of the British Railways and the London Transport Railways (*A.A.S.*, Tables 241 and 247).

TABLE 14

Purchased Transport and Communications

	Thai		U.K.		£ million			
	Q	P (£ per unit)	Q	P (£ per unit)	$P_T Q_T$	$P_U Q_U$	$P_T Q_U$	$P_U Q_T$
Public road passenger vehicles (000 vehicles)	36·5	2·06	96	5125	75	492	198	184
Railroad (000 million passenger—kilometres)	2·7	0·0040	35·7	0·0060	11	202	245	16
Telephone and telegraph (million calls)	110·5	0·0159	5300	0·0166	1·8	88	84	1·8
Letters posted (million)	67·6	0·0125	10·6	0·0125	0·8	133	133	0·8
			Total: £ million		89·6	915	560	192·6
			Total: £ per head		3·07	17·05	10·43	6·66

$$\frac{\Sigma P_{iU} Q_{iU}}{\Sigma P_{iU} Q_{iT}} = 2\cdot56 \qquad \frac{\Sigma P_{iT} Q_{iU}}{\Sigma P_{iT} Q_{iT}} = 3\cdot40 \qquad \text{Fisher index} = 2\cdot95$$

$$\frac{\Sigma P_{iU} Q_{iU}}{\Sigma P_{iT} Q_{iT}} = 5\cdot55$$

The totals in Table 14 are probably overestimates of the values appropriate for Table 10 because some of the services of each means of transport and communication are performed for firms rather than for final consumers, and because some of the consumer's expenditure on transport should be attributed to 'transport to work', which is a cost of production, or intermediate produce paid for by consumers. Nevertheless totals in Table 14 are reproduced unchanged in Table 10. The net effect of the bias is almost certainly to make the U.K. appear relatively more prosperous.

(f) AUTOMOBILES, NOT USED FOR PUBLIC TRANSPORT

The purchase and running cost of cars owned and driven by people who are not in the business of transport is distinguished in Table 10 from purchased transport to emphasize a difference in Thai and British consumption patterns. The British use 2·5 times as much purchased transport as the Thai, but the British own and buy almost fifty times as many automobiles for private use.

Following the practice in the national accounts of both countries, the purchase of automobiles is included as a consumption good rather than as an investment. To measure the services of existing stock of automobiles, it is supposed that the real service per automobile is the same in both countries, and that the value of the services of automobiles corresponds to the item 'running costs' in the national accounts.

Stocks of automobiles are from the statistical abstracts (*A.A.S.*, Table 232, vehicles with licences current, 'Private cars', and 'Motor cycles, etc.'; and *S.Y.T.*, Table 122, Motor Vehicle Registration, 'Personal cars'). Numbers of automobiles and motor cycles purchased in Thailand are estimated by the Thai National Income Office from statistics of imports; the comparable British figure is new registrations (*A.A.S.*, Table 233, 'Cars, etc.' and 'Motor cycles, etc.'). Motor cycles are counted in Table 15 as 0·2 automobiles in purchase and 0·112 in running cost, corresponding to relative prices in the Thai accounts (*N.I.T.*, Table 20, item 10a, 'Personal transport equipment', and item 10b 'Operation of personal transport equipment'; and *N.I.E.*, Table 18, 'Durable goods: motor cars and motor cycles' and 'Running cost of motor vehicles').

TABLE 15

Private Automobiles

	Thailand		U.K.		£ million			
	Q	P	Q	P	$P_T Q_T$	$P_U Q_U$	$P_T Q_U$	$P_U Q_T$
purchase of new automobiles ('000)	16·78	651	1046	602	10·9	630	681	10·1
the services of automobiles (Q measured as the number of automobiles in thousands)	61·59	82	7744	82	5·1	635	635	5·1
Total: £ million					15·0	1265	1316	15·2
Total: £ per head					0·52	23·59	24·52	0·53

$$\frac{\Sigma P_U Q_U}{\Sigma P_T Q_T} = 45 \cdot 33 \qquad \frac{\Sigma P_T Q_U}{\Sigma P_T Q_T} = 46 \cdot 52 \qquad \frac{\Sigma P_U Q_U}{\Sigma P_U Q_T} = 44 \cdot 75 \qquad \text{Fisher index} = 45 \cdot 63$$

(g) OTHER DURABLES

Because we cannot break down values of other durables into prices and quantities, and because consumer durables in Thailand include imported items that are relatively expensive and domestically produced items that are relatively cheap, it is supposed that prices of 'other durables' are on the average the same in Thailand and the United Kingdom in the sense that the exchange rate represents a purchasing power parity. For Thailand, 'other durables' comprises 'Furniture, furnishings, and household equipment' (*N.I.T.*, Table 20, item 7) and for the U.K., 'other durables' comprises 'Durable goods: furniture and floor coverings', 'Durable goods: radio, electrical, and other durable goods', and 'Other miscellaneous goods' (*N.I.E.*, Table 18).

(h) PERSONAL CARE AND MISCELLANEOUS HOUSEHOLD EXPENDITURE

Items under this heading in the British national accounts are 'Chemists goods', 'Other household goods', and 'Hairdressing'. Values of the first two items are from Table 18 of *N.I.E.* The value of hairdressing included in the U.K. accounts in the general category 'Other services', is estimated from a statistic for the year 1954 in *National Income Statistics: Sources and Methods* (H.M.S.O. 1956) by supposing that the value of hairdressing increases over time in proportion to the national income as a whole. The corresponding value in the Thai accounts is 'personal care' (item 9a, Table 20, *N.I.T.*).

In passing from $P_T O_T$ and $P_U Q_U$ to $P_T Q_U$ and $P_U Q_T$ in Table 10, it is assumed that the Thai price level is one third of the British price level. This is done for two reasons, neither very strong or very satisfying. One of the larger items in this category is haircuts. The price of a man's haircut is 4 baht in Thailand and 4 shillings in the United Kingdom, and the exchange rate between bahts and shillings is about three to one. Second, as most of the items in this category are domestically produced, it seems reasonable to suppose that the ratio of Thai to British price levels in this category of goods is not very different from the ratio of price levels in the economies as a whole. Column 7 of the bottom row of Table 10 shows this to be about a third.

(i) DOMESTIC SERVICE

The number of man-years of domestic service in the United Kingdom is estimated by dividing the value of domestic service in the national accounts (*N.I.E.*, Table 18, 'Domestic services') by an assumed wage of £300 a year. The figure of £300 was chosen to be consistent with the estimate of £200 for 1948 in *National Income Statistics: Sources and Methods* (H.M.S.O., 1956). The Thai National Income Office estimated the number of servants at 72 000 by supposing that 1·5 per cent of all Thai households keep a servant and that households contain six people on the average. A typical servant's wage, inclusive of board, is about 200 baht a month or £41·38 a year.

(j) RECREATION

The value of 'recreation' in Thailand is the sum of the values of 'Entertainment', 'Books, newspapers, and magazines', and 'Other recreation' in *N.I.T.* (Table 20, items 11a, 11c, and 11d). The corresponding value in the U.K. is the sum of the values of 'Books, newspapers, and magazines', 'Miscellaneous recreational goods', and 'Entertainments' in *N.I.E.* (Table 18). Since there are no independent estimates of prices or quantities, the Thai price of 'recreation' is assumed to be a third of the British price, in accordance with price levels for incomes as a whole.

(k) HEALTH

Medical services are compared in Table 16 under the headings of doctors and dentists, pharmaceuticals, and numbers of hospital beds, the last item being a surrogate for all medical services other than doctors, dentists, and pharmaceuticals. The numbers of Thai doctors and dentists is from the files of the National Income Office. There are 4440 doctors trained in modern medicine and 33 900 doctors trained in Thai indigenous medicine. In estimating a number of doctors in Thailand suitable for comparison with the number of doctors in the U.K., doctors trained in modern medicine are given a weight of unity and doctors trained in indigenous medicine are given a weight of one-tenth corresponding to the estimate of the National Income Office of their relative incomes. The price of doctors' services in Thailand is imputed by dividing

TABLE 16

Health

	Thailand		U.K.		£ million			
	Q	P imputed	Q	P imputed	P_TQ_T	P_UQ_U	P_TQ_U	P_UQ_T
doctors and dentists	8979	764	57 576	2900	6·86	167·0	57·6	26·09
pharmaceuticals					20·00	123·8	123·8	20·00
hospital beds	1480	336	551 000	1053	5·07	580·2	187·3	15·54
Total: £ million					31·93	871·0	368·7	61·58
Total: £ per head					1·11	16·22	6·87	2·14

$$\frac{\Sigma P_{iU}Q_{iU}}{\Sigma P_{iT}Q_{iT}} = 14\cdot61$$

$$\frac{\Sigma P_{iU}Q_{iU}}{\Sigma P_{iU}Q_{iT}} = 7\cdot58$$

$$\frac{\Sigma P_{iT}Q_{iU}}{\Sigma P_{iT}Q_{iT}} = 6\cdot19$$

the quantity into the total value. Numbers of doctors and dentists and public expenditure on doctors and dentists in the United Kingdom are from *A.A.S.* (Tables 49–51); the U.K. expenditure includes only that of the Hospital Services and of the Executive Council Services.

Pharmaceutical costs are from the files of the Thai National Income Office, from the statement of the cost of drugs to hospitals in the *Annual Report of the Ministry of Health* 1964, H.M.S.O. (Table 74) and from the statement of gross payments to pharmacists under the Executive Council Services in *A.A.S.* (Tables 49–51). It is supposed that pharmaceutical prices are the same in Thailand and the United Kingdom.

Numbers of hospital beds are from *S.Y.T.* (Table 37) and *A.A.S.* (Tables 49–51). Costs of hospital services, exclusive of payments to doctors, and the cost of drugs are from the files of the Thai National Income Office and *A.A.S.* (Tables 49–51).

(l) EDUCATION

It is supposed that real educational services may be compared as ratios of numbers of teachers employed, with teachers in primary schools, secondary and other schools, and universities given weights of unity, two, and four respectively. Numbers of teachers are from *S.Y.T.* (Tables 52 and 60) and from *A.A.* (Tables 89, 101, and 108). Ratios of numbers of teachers in the three classes are as 1:0·49:0·07 in the United Kingdom and as 1:0·08:0·025 in Thailand. Values of education are from *N.I.E.* (Table 42, 'Analysis of current expenditure on goods and services. Combined Public Authorities, Social services: Education') and from *N.I.T.* (Table 21, 'Composition of General Government Consumption Expenditure. By Purpose Education and Research').

(m) INSURANCE AND CONSUMER EXPENDITURE ABROAD

Values in these categories are from *N.I.E.* (Table 18), from *N.I.T.* (Table 20) and from data on insurance in the files of the Thai National Income Office. Insurance includes only the cost of administering insurance companies, and not the value of the premiums. Price levels in these categories are assumed to be the same in both countries. Following the British practice, the services of banks are not included on the expenditure side of national income.

(n) LEGAL AND RELIGIOUS SERVICES

Numbers of lawyers and monks in Thailand are from the files of the Thai National Income Office, and from *S.Y.T.* (Table 214). Numbers of lawyers, including barristers, judges, and solicitors, and of monks, nuns, and ministers of religion in the United Kingdom are computed from figures in the census by increasing the figures in proportion to the rise of population between the date of the census and 1963.

Income of lawyers and ministers in the United Kingdom are assumed to be £3000 and £1000 respectively. Services of lawyers are valued at only half their incomes on the assumption that these services are apportioned equally between final consumers and firms; services to firms are intermediate products excluded from national income. Incomes of Thai lawyers are estimated by the Thai National Income Office. Services of monks cannot be measured by their incomes because the rules of the Buddhist religion place the monks outside the market sector. An income of £25 per man is imputed; this income is somewhat less than the value of consumption per head in the country as a whole but well above the value of food consumption.

The services of Thai monks are partly religious and partly educational. It is customary for all Thai men to spend three months during their lives in a monastery as an advanced form of character training. It is the social function of the permanent monks to make this possible. Only numbers of permanent monks are recorded in Table 17. Even the meditation of the monks is thought to confer benefit on the community as a whole, and it is not for the statistician to question the values of the community as to what is income and what is not.

(o) PUBLIC ADMINISTRATION

The number of civil servants is treated as a measure of the services of public administration. The number of Thai civil servants is estimated as the economically active population in the category of services and in the employ of the government (*S.Y.T.*, Table 20) *less* the number of employees in the Ministries of Public Health, and Education (*S.Y.T.*, Table 195). The number of

TABLE 17

Legal and Religious Services

| | Thai | | U.K. | | £ thousand | | | |
	Q (number)	P (income per man)	Q (number)	P (income per man)	$P_T Q_T$	$P_U Q_U$	$P_T Q_U$	$P_U Q_T$
law ministers and monks	3729	150	29 567	1500	559	44 351	4435	5594
	150 685	25	61 175	1000	3767	61 175	1529	150 685
	Total: £ thousand				4326	105 526	5964	156 279
	Total: £ per head				0·15	1·97	0·11	5·42

$$\frac{\Sigma P_{iU} Q_{iU}}{\Sigma P_{iT} Q_{iT}} = 13 \cdot 13 \qquad \frac{\Sigma P_{iU} Q_{iU}}{\Sigma P_{iU} Q_{iT}} = 0 \cdot 36 \qquad \frac{\Sigma P_{iT} Q_{iU}}{\Sigma P_{iT} Q_{iT}} = 0 \cdot 74$$

Fisher index = 0·52

British civil servants is estimated as the total labour force in public administration in national and local government (*A.A.S.*, Table 130) *less* the non-industrial staff in the civil service under the headings of post office, defence, and supply departments, the Department of Education and Science, and the Ministry of Health. Defined in this peculiar way, the number of civil servants in Thailand and the United Kingdom are 261 thousand and 947 thousand respectively.

The values of public administration are defined as government consumption expenditure less military expenditure and expenditures on health and education. The value in the United Kingdom is the total 'Current expenditure on goods and services' of the 'Combined Public Authorities' *less* expenditure on 'Defence' and 'Social services; Education, and the National Health Service' (*N.I.E.*, Table 42). The value of public administration in Thailand is 'General government consumption expenditure' *less* expenditure on 'Defence', 'Education and research', and 'Health services'.

Education and health are left out of public administration because they appear elsewhere in the accounts. Defence is left out because Thailand does not publish statistics on numbers of soldiers and because local expenditure cannot be extricated from foreign aid in a satisfactory way.

(p) NET CAPITAL FORMATION

Net capital formation in the United Kingdom is from *N.I.E.* (Table 66), and net capital formation in Thailand is estimated by reducing gross capital formation recorded in *N.I.T.* (Table 19, item 3), by the proportion between net and gross capital formation in the United Kingdom. Prices of capital goods in the two countries are assumed to be the same. Half of Thai gross capital formation consists of imports, c.i.f. of capital goods including industrial raw materials, import duties make up another 15 per cent, leaving 35 per cent attributable to local costs and expenditures. Imported items are presumably more expensive in Thailand than in the United Kingdom but local capital formation is probably cheaper.

14

The Chain of Prices:
Rice Prices from the Thai Farmer
to the British Consumer

So far we have examined the kinds of forces that might hold apart price levels in different places, and have tried to measure the total gap between price levels in Thailand and the U.K. But we have not yet attempted to distribute the total price gap among its components, domestic transport cost, international transport cost, tariffs, and the pricing of untraded products, or to measure the relative magnitudes of the forces holding price levels apart. That is the task of this chapter. An attempt is made to attach numbers to the chain of prices described qualitatively in Chapter 6.

The information may be useful in several ways. Our main concern is to use the chain of prices in assessing the relative importance of the forces tending to depress the money incomes of the poor countries. There are, however, two substantial by-products of the information. First, it serves as a check on the statistics of the total price gaps presented in the previous chapter. The figure of 359 per cent as the total price gap for cereals seems at first glance to be larger than might be accounted for by the normal cost of trade. A breakdown of the total gap into its components can reveal whether this is so. Second, the chain of prices is an aid in assessing efficiency of the trade and distribution sectors of an economy. It is frequently said of underdeveloped countries that farmers get low prices for their products because they are systematically cheated by middlemen who impose an unconscionably large margin between farm prices and retail prices or export prices. The chain of prices cannot in itself establish conclusively whether a margin is reasonable or not, but it does show the maximum benefit a farmer might expect from a reduction in the cost of trade.[1]

In principle it is a simple matter to collect a chain of prices. One visits markets, observes buying and selling prices, and asks traders about their normal costs and profits. In practice this type of investigation is very time-consuming, and consequently this chapter is limited to the study of a single commodity, rice, chosen because it is on almost any standard the most important commodity in the Thai economy. The study may be looked upon as a prototype that reveals the problems encountered in forcing the raw data of the market into our theoretical scheme, and in interpreting the results.

Table 18 is a summary of the chain of prices. Starting from the Thai farmer, two lines of trade are shown, export to the U.K. on the right and retail sale in Thailand on the left. The main aggregates of cost are shown in individual boxes; the percentages to the right of each box are of the Thai retail price. The sum of the values in the boxes in each column totals to the retail price shown in the lowest box. This table differs from the theoretical scheme in Part II in that the chain of prices in the export trade starts with the Thai farm price which is lower than the Thai retail price, and in the inclusion of blocks representing the cost of processing. For simplicity, it was supposed in Part II that goods are first made and then traded in a form suitable for final consumption. In fact, rice is physically altered between stages of distribution; it is milled and placed in sacks in Thailand, and cleaned and put into cartons in England. Processing and distribution are distinguished in the table even though the exact dividing line is not always clear.

The table leaves no doubt that the over-all differential in rice prices between Thailand and the U.K. is consistent with the ratio (359 per cent) of cereal prices calculated in the previous chapter. The English retail price of rice is 492 per cent of the Thai retail price and 623 per cent of the Thai farm price; the most likely the explanation of why these figures are higher than 359 per cent is that rice was equated, calorie for calorie, to English bread and potatoes, both considerably cheaper than rice in the

---

[1] The use of the chain of prices as an indicator of efficiency will not be examined here, for it is the subject of 'The Thai Rice Trade', a chapter in *Thailand Social and Economic Studies in Development* edited by T. Silcock (Australian National University Press, 1967). The reader may consult that book for greater detail on the rice trade and for general information on the Thai economy.

T<small>ABLE</small> 18

Summary of the Chain of Rice Prices in Thailand and the U.K.

Rice sold retail at Bangkok   *Rice exported to England*

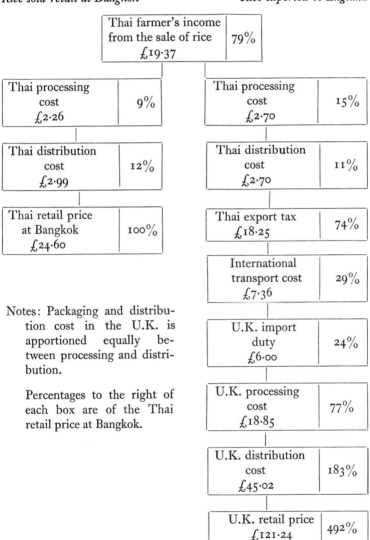

| Thai farmer's income from the sale of rice £19·37 | 79% |

| Thai processing cost £2·26 | 9% | Thai processing cost £2·70 | 15% |

| Thai distribution cost £2·99 | 12% | Thai distribution cost £2·70 | 11% |

| Thai retail price at Bangkok £24·60 | 100% | Thai export tax £18·25 | 74% |

| | | International transport cost £7·36 | 29% |

Notes: Packaging and distribution cost in the U.K. is apportioned equally between processing and distribution.

| | | U.K. import duty £6·00 | 24% |

| | | U.K. processing cost £18·85 | 77% |

Percentages to the right of each box are of the Thai retail price at Bangkok.

| | | U.K. distribution cost £45·02 | 183% |

| | | U.K. retail price £121·24 | 492% |

U.K. The Thai farmer gets less than a sixth of the retail price of rice in the U.K.; he gets less for growing rice than the English retailer gets for selling it, less than the cost of English wholesale distribution, and only slightly more than the export tax imposed by the Thai Government.

HOW THE CHAIN OF PRICES WAS COMPILED

Data on rice prices and traders' costs in Table 18 were collected in interviews with people in the trade. Farmers, millers, crop buyers, truckers, retailers, and exporters were asked about buying and selling prices and about the normal costs of conducting business. Where possible their data were checked against official price statistics of the Thai government. The chain of prices could not be constructed entirely from the official statistics, because prices are not collected at all stages of trade and because the official indices, designed to show major price fluctuations over time, are often insufficiently sensitive to differences in qualities of rice, locations, or day-to-day fluctuations in prices.

The raw data have been put through two stages of condensation in the compilation of Table 18. Table 19 presents data of the Thai rice trade approximately as they were collected while Table 20 aggregates the Thai data and adds information about the import and distribution of rice in the U.K.

Table 19 is supposed to represent a typical pattern of prices and mark-ups from the farm to the final sale in Thailand, retail in Bangkok or for export. Each number in the table has been cross-checked in interviews with at least a dozen business men in the appropriate branch of the trade. There was no fixed rule about who or how many people to interview but eventually a pattern of costs and prices would emerge.

In a programme of investigation based on a limited number of interviews in circumstances where incorrect information appears from time to time due to misunderstandings or to deliberate deception (for traders were sometimes asked about facts that they would prefer not to reveal), it is inevitable that the interviewer must judge what is true and what is false, what is typical and what is not, and he must to some extent impose his own standards of reasonableness onto the data. Certainly the facts of the trade are not as neat or as orderly as the data in Table 19. But I think the

TABLE 19 *An Example of the Chain of Rice in Thailand*
(Prices and costs of one ton of paddy yielding mainly 100 per cent quality rice, milled about 30 km from Bangkok, February 1965)

Rice sold to Thai consumers at Bangkok				*Rice exported*		
% of Bangkok retail price	Price of rice	Costs		Costs	Price of rice	% of export price f.o.b.
79	770		paddy price at the farm		770	46
3		30	transport to the mill	30		2
			The miller's costs			
82	800		paddy price at the mill		800	48
	expenses when rice is sold at the mill		unloading 5 / labour 35 / tax 35 / profit 12 unloading 5 / labour 35 / tax 36 / transport to Bangkok 18 / commission 5 / other selling expenses 10 / profit 12	expenses when rice is sold in Bangkok		
9		87	total milling cost	121		8

The miller's income

rice sold at the mill *baht*		milling out-turn		rice sold at Bangkok *baht*	
value	per kg.	grade of rice	kg.	per kg.	value
650	1·57	100%	420	1·62	680
38	0·92	A1 spec.	42	0·97	41
139	0·82	A1	170	0·87	148
23	0·57	C1	40	0·62	25
27	0·30	bran	90	—	—

% of Bangkok retail price	Price of rice	Costs		Costs	Price of rice	% of export price f.o.b.
88	860		price of rice sold at the mill wholesale price of rice sold at Bangkok		894	54
3	27		price of bran sold at the mill		27	2
2		18	transport charges (per sack of 100 kg, 1 truck 1·5, loading and unloading 0·5 each) export tax (4·2%) ... rice premium	69 / 631		4 / 38
7		67	retail markup (10 baht per sack of 100 kg) exporter's gross margin (60 baht per ton)	40		2
	945		Bangkok selling price of rice selling price of rice f.o.b.		1634	
100	972		rice price inclusive of the value of the bran sold at the mill		1661	100

table conveys the general picture correctly. The danger of the
interviewer distorting the data was reduced considerably by the fact
that one could always question both sides of the market; the selling
price of one trader is the buying price of the next: the selling
price of the farmer is the buying price of the middleman; the
selling price of the middleman is the buying price of the miller;
and so on.

Table 19 is to a great extent based on information provided by
a miller whose pattern of costs and prices seemed to be typical of
the milling trade as a whole. Prices quoted in the right hand side
of the miller's income statement are actual Bangkok prices. The
paddy price checked with what farmers in the area said they were
paid for their rice. The item 'transport to the mill' records the cost
of bringing rice from the farm to the mill. Sometimes the miller
does this himself, in which case his gross profit per ton is higher
than is shown in the table. More often, this stage of the rice trade is
conducted by specialists. Below the miller's accounts, the table
breaks into left and right halves, showing mark-ups in the retail
and export trades. The 'rice premium' is an export tax distinguished from the item above it because it is levied per ton
exported rather than in proportion to value.

The main problem in transforming Table 19 into Table 20 was
to decide what constitutes rice. The Thai farmer sells paddy, one
metric ton of which is milled into 672 kilograms of rice of various
grades as shown in Table 19. The low grades are not imported
into England, but one cannot say what proportion of the British
price the Thai farmer gets unless some account is taken of the low
grades as well as of the high grades. Consequently, it was supposed that the whole mix of rice derived from a ton of paddy is
shipped to the U.K. Bran, on the other hand, is assumed to be sold
in Thailand. In passing from Table 19 to Table 20, the paddy price
is reduced by the price of bran so that all of the numbers in Table
20 refer to rice only. The English data in Table 20 were furnished
by traders in London.

The derivation of Table 18 from Tables 19 and 20 is largely
self-explanatory. Numbers pertaining to the Thai retail trade are
converted into £ per long ton from Table 19 and numbers pertaining to the export trade are from Table 20. Processing cost is
the only tricky item. In the Thai retail trade, it includes only the
cost of milling, and in the Thai export trade it includes the cost

of milling (net of transport to Bangkok) plus the cost of jute bags. In the U.K., processing includes packaging, cleaning, fumigation, new bags, and weight loss in ocean transport and in England. Weight loss is not really a cost because it does not correspond to the income of any factor of production, but it does contribute to the price gap. Weight loss is included with processing to separate it from other items that are of more direct interest to us.

In addition to technical problems of collecting data and assembling them into a chain of prices—problems of interviewing, of sifting true responses from false ones, of averaging observations, etc.—there are difficulties of a more fundamental kind that arise because the notion of a chain of prices of a major commodity like rice requires that some complexities of the market be overlooked. The chain of prices can be rigorously defined with respect to a perfectly homogeneous commodity that moves from one location to another at a moment of time. A grain of rice has one price where it is grown, another where it is sold retail, and a series of prices in between. But to speak of the chain of rice prices between Thailand and the U.K. without exact reference to the variety of rice, the locations in Thailand and in the U.K., or the date, is to overlook the fact that these conditions influence the chain of prices. In introducing Table 18 it was claimed that the chain of prices was typical of the country as a whole. An attempt will now be made to assess the extent to which numbers would have to be changed if a different example had been chosen.

Examining the items in Table 20, we see that most originate in money terms, baht per ton or £ per ton, but that some originate as percentages of the rice price. If all items originated in money terms, a change in the price of rice[1] would leave the chain of prices invariant in money terms but not as a percentage of the price at any stage of trade. If all items originated as percentages of the rice price, a change in the world price of rice would leave the chain of prices invariant as percentages of the rice price at any stage of trade but not in money terms. Since some items originate as percentages and others in fixed money terms, a change in the rice price necessarily affects the chain of prices no matter how it is recorded. An increase in the rice price causes the gap between prices in Thailand and the U.K. to widen in money terms but to

[1] In this context a change in the rice price should be understood as a change in prices everywhere, as recorded in any commodity market.

TABLE 20

The Chain of Rice Prices from the Thai Farmer to the English Consumer, February 1965

The ton of paddy yielded 672 kg rice	*Baht per metric ton of paddy*	*£ per long ton of rice*
Farm price (paddy rice less the price of bran)	743	19·37
Middleman	30	0·78
Paddy price at mill	773	20·15
Miller's gross margin	121	3·15
Bangkok wholesale price	894	23·31
jute bags (a bag for 100 kg of rice cost 8 baht)	54	1·41
Export tax and rice premium	700	18·25
Exporters expense and profit	40	1·04
f.o.b. Bangkok baht per ton of paddy	1688	44·01
f.o.b. Bangkok per metric ton of rice ($£1 = 58$ baht)	*£ per metric ton of rice*	
	43·31	44·01
Charge of European exporter (-/2/6 per metric ton)	0·125	0·127
Quality survey (-/2/6 per metric ton)	0·125	0·127
Freight	6·5	6·60
Interest ($\frac{1}{2}$%) insurance ($\frac{1}{2}$%) weight loss (1%)	1·00	1·02
C.i.f. London (1 long ton = 2240 lb; 1 metric ton = 2204·62 lb)	51·06	51·88
U.K. tariff		6·00
U.K. landing charge		2·95
Cleaning (£4) fumigation (£0/5) new bags £1/15)		6·00
Rent of warehouse (inc. transport etc)		1·00
Weight loss in cleaning (1%)		0·68
Total cost of rice wholesale		68·51
Packaging and distribution (each $1\frac{1}{4}$ per lb)		23·33
Gross profit of importer and wholesaler (10%)		9·19
Price to shop		101·03
Shop margin (20%)		20·21
Retail price £-/1/1 per lb)		121·24

become narrower when recorded as a percentage of any particular rice price.

The exact, geographical origin of the rice in Thailand makes surprisingly little difference to the chain of prices. With a few minor exceptions, the direction of the rice trade in Thailand is south to Bangkok from the wedge-shaped area to the north and east, and south from Bangkok through the long peninsula that eventually becomes Malaysia. Rice prices decrease continually from north to south, but the amount of the decrease is small because the transport within Thailand is cheap.

Some observations on transport costs are shown on Graph 2. The vertical axis shows the rate per metric ton for a given journey and the horizontal axis shows the length of the journey. Both axes are graduated on a log scale to condense the right hand side of the graph and to enable transport cost per ton kilometre to be shown by parallel straight lines slanted at 45 degrees. It may be seen at once from these lines that transport costs per ton-kilometre vary fiftyfold, the cheapest transport being by canal boat over long distances and the most expensive being by ox-cart. Ox-carts are only used to carry small loads of paddy from farms to nearby mills; they would be completely uneconomical on long hauls.

Most transport of grain over long distances is by truck, rail, or canal boat. The example of Table 19 is of rice originating 30 kilometres north of Bangkok and carried to Bangkok by truck at a cost of 15 baht per ton, exclusive of loading and unloading charges which are the same no matter how far the rice is carried. Almost half the rice in Thailand is grown within a radius of 100 kilometres of Bangkok, where the cost of transport to Bangkok does not exceed 50 baht per ton. The highest transport rates recorded under normal road conditions are about 125 baht for a distance of 700 kilometres. Since the Bangkok price of rice is fixed by conditions in the world market, the effect of extra transport cost is to lower the farm price. If the transport cost were 125 baht instead of 15 baht in the example in Table 19, the farm price of paddy would fall to 669 baht,[1] the miller's buying and selling prices would be reduced by the amount of the extra transport cost, and the rest of the chain of prices would remain the same.

[1] The extra transport cost would be only 74 baht per ton of paddy because a ton of paddy yields only 0·672 tons of rice. Normally a farmer sends his paddy to a nearby mill.

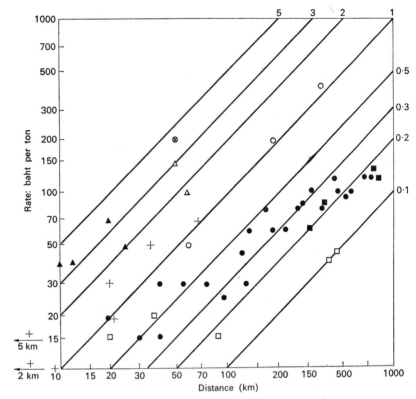

The diagonal lines trace out points of equal rate per unit
distance (baht per ton-kilometer, as indicated at the top of each line).

● trucking on public roads (rice in sacks)   □ boat (paddy)

○ trucking on public roads -dirt roads in very poor   ▲ ox-cart (carries only 1/2 ton)
  condition (rice in sacks)   △ jeep (carries one ton)

■ rail road, door to door including ETO service
  (rice in sacks)

⊗ small boat, up stream in rainy season

+ either millers reduction in the price of paddy for
  collecting paddy at the farm, or commercial trucking
  rate for that service

GRAPH 2. Transport cost in Thailand, February–March 1965.

The chain of prices in Table 18 was compiled for a specific date,
February 1965, and for a specific quality of rice, the mix described
in Table 19. A change in either the date of the table or the quality
of rice would alter the table substantially, the former because
prices of all grades of rice fluctuate greatly over time and the latter

because quality differences are recognized in the structure of rice prices at any time. The miller's income statement shows rice prices in Bangkok varying by almost three fold, from 0·57 baht per kilogram for grade C_1, which is rice so broken that it is almost powder, to 1·57 baht per kilogram for '100 per cent rice' which, as its name implies, is virtually perfect rice with unbroken grains of the right biological variety, size, shape, colour, etc. Measured as a percentage of the Thai farmer's price, the total price gap in Table 18 would have been smaller than shown if the computation had been exclusively for '100 per cent' rice, and the total price gap would have been larger if the computation had been for rice of grade C_1.

Time affects rice prices in two ways. There is the normal day-to-day and year-to-year variation in prices. The price of rice costing, for instance, 150 baht per 100 kilograms at moment of time might easily vary by 40 baht from one year to the next, and day to day fluctuations of 5 baht are common. A change in rice prices between two periods of time affects the chain of prices in the same way that a change in the grade of rice affects the chain of prices at a moment of time.

The other effect of time on rice prices is in causing storage and interest changes. Most of the Thai rice crop is harvested in October and November, and must be stored so that rice may be consumed all year round. Table 18 was compiled without storage or interest charges; it was supposed that rice was bought from the farmer, milled, and exported quickly. The reasons for excluding these items are that a great deal of the rice exported from Thailand is shipped out soon after the harvest, that is not clear how long a period of storage should be allowed for, and that the storage and interest charge might have been added to the cost of any of the Thai traders, for farmers, millers, and exporters all store rice from time to time. Nevertheless, the exclusion of storage and interest charges has biased down the estimate of the Thai distribution cost. Taking low and high grades of rice together, the annual appreciation of the rice price is about 15 per cent.[1] If the average period of storage over the year were four months (it would be less than six months

[1] The gradual appreciation of the rice price over the year is of particular interest because it provides an indicator of the effective short-term rate of interest in the business community. Old rice (rice stored for a year) is considered superior in quality to new rice (rice of the most recent harvest). The difference between the prices of old and new rice adjusted for the cost of storage and

because the export of rice is concentrated in the period after the harvest and because there is some doubling-cropping), an extra 5 per cent of the Thai farm price at harvest time would have to be added to the Thai distribution cost.[1]

THE RELATIVE IMPORTANCE OF BIASES IN INCOME COMPARISON

Even a chain of prices for one commodity provides ground for speculation about the contribution of each of the biases discussed in Part II to the total differential between the price levels in Thailand and the U.K. Part of the disadvantage of having only one commodity is compensated for by the overriding importance of rice in the Thai economy. Since rice is at once the staple food, the principle product, and the major export of Thailand, changes in the rice price are communicated to prices of many other products through their substitutability for rice in production, in use, or in competition for labour. The rice price is a major determinant of the whole price level. This point will be elaborated in the next chapter.

On examining the components of the chain of prices in Table 18 we see that almost half of the gap between the Thai and U.K. retail prices is accounted for by distribution cost and there is a marked contrast between costs in the two countries. The Thai distribution cost from the farmer to the urban consumer is £2·99 per long ton; the U.K. distribution cost from the first appearance of rice in the U.K. to its final sale to British consumers is £45·02 per long ton. If we may suppose that the services of distribution per ton of rice are more or less the same in the two situations, it follows that the ratio of the prices of distribution in the U.K. and in Thailand is about 15 to 1, a ratio more or less comparable to the ratios of prices of other direct personal services, domestic service, legal and religious services, and education, shown in the far right-hand column of the summary table, Table 10, of the previous

---

insurance, and expressed as a percentage of the price of new rice, is a measure of the interest rate, which turns out to be about 10 per cent per annum, rather lower than rates in underdeveloped countries are believed to be but consistent with many other facts about the Thai economy. The steps in the calculation are described in 'Thai Interest Rates', *Journal of Development Studies*, April 1967.

[1] The sizeable random fluctuation in the rice price over time generates large windfall gains or losses to traders storing rice. In constructing Tables 18, 19, and 20, these windfall gains or losses were assumed to cancel out.

chapter. The difference between Thai and U.K. distribution costs might be explained as a compound of three elements:

(a) It is unlikely that there is much difference in the efficiency of labour in the Thai and U.K. distribution systems. Both use trucks in transport. The Thai rice shop is not unlike the English corner grocery and, in both countries, retail trade accounts for about half of the total distribution cost.

(b) Since the U.K. price level is higher than the Thai price level, the income of people engaged in distribution must be higher in the U.K. than in Thailand if people engaged in distribution are to be equally well off.

(c) The higher standard of living in the U.K. resulting from the greater productivity of manufacturing in the U.K. is shared by people engaged in providing services such as retail distribution, and the mechanism by which this comes about is that the price of services in the U.K. is higher relative to the price of goods— exactly the process described in Chapter 8, on the pricing of untraded products.

The analysis of the price mechanism in Part II showed how price gaps could affect the measurement of income. The casual connection was from international transport costs, from tariffs set by the governments, or from fixed costs of trade, to biases in income comparisons. The opposite tendency is at work in the formation of rice prices in Thailand and the U.K. Differences between the countries in price levels and in living standards have a substantial effect on the price gap. In reality, the causal connection works both ways. Price gaps affect comparative price levels and are affected by them, as illustrated in the model of internal transport cost in Chapter 10, where the price differentials between the farms and the city were determined jointly by the technology of transport, given outside the economic system, and the real wage, established as part of the full general equilibrium.

It appears that neither international transport cost nor domestic transport cost can influence the national incomes very much. International transport cost amounts to a third of the Thai farm price; the Thai rice price would rise by no more than a third if international transport were free. But for international transport cost to depress the whole Thai price level in the way described in Chapter 9 it is necessary either that the transport cost of Thai imports is very much lower than the transport cost of Thai exports, or that Thai imports are primarily semi-finished products, or that Thai imports are products that do not enter significantly into the cost of living. Though all three of these conditions characterize the Thai economy to some extent, I doubt that even their combined effect is to depress the Thai price level very much. Thai domestic transport is quite cheap and U.K. domestic transport seems to be a relatively small part of the total distribution cost. It is unlikely that there would be any significant difference between price levels in Thailand and the U.K. if transport cost on traded products were the only source of the difference.

A considerably larger share of the total price gap may be accounted for by the combined effect of the Thai export tax and the U.K. import duty. Together these amount to about 125 per cent of the Thai farm price. If price levels in Thailand and the U.K. adjusted themselves to keep grain wages more or less as they are now, abolition of these two taxes could double the apparent real income of Thailand, in £ per head.

In a rough and approximate way, the biases in the income comparison in money terms may be listed in order of importance; first the pricing of untraded products including distribution cost, then trade taxes, then international transport cost, and finally domestic transport cost. Unlike the components of the price gap, the biases in income comparison are not additive, but more like equations that fit into a system. Though observed transport costs are small, it is the potentially exorbitant transport cost on untraded products that keep these products out of international trade. Tariffs depress the rice price, keeping money wages down, and this in turn depresses prices of untraded products and of services including the services of distribution. One cannot allocate percentages of the total price gap among the causes, because the effect of each cause depends upon the rest. But there are more precise questions that do admit numerical answers. It might be asked what the effect would be on the Thai price level or productivity statistics of an abolition of the export tax on rice. To answer this question it is necessary to trace the effects of a change in the rice price on other prices and on the physical composition of the national output. Though we do not have all the information needed to answer this question accurately, an approximate answer can be got with the data at hand. This is attempted in the next chapter.

15

Income as a Measure of Productivity: Alternative Comparisons of Agricultural and Non-Agricultural Productivity in Thailand

PRODUCTIVITY statistics are right or wrong, accurate or inaccurate only with reference to the context where they are used. They are right or accurate if they bear the implications attributed to them. The context in which we shall evaluate Thai productivity statistics is the debate in the economic literature about the alleged justification for a tariff on manufactures as a means of diverting labour from agriculture where its productivity is low to other sectors where its productivity is higher.[1] The discussion of this issue[2] has concentrated on the major premise of the argument, namely that if productivity of agriculture is low, then tariffs may be beneficial. We are concerned with the minor premise. We propose to examine the usual measure of productivity of agriculture to see if the statistics really bear the implications attributed to them in the policy discussion.[3]

The productivity statistics cited as evidence in this discussion are those showing income per man employed by industry,[4] computed

[1] E. E. Hagen, 'An Economic Justification of Protectionism', *Quarterly Journal of Economics*, November 1958.

[2] See for instance J. Bhagwati and V. K. Ramaswami, 'Domestic Distortions, Tariffs and the Theory of Optimum Subsidy', *Journal of Political Economy*, February 1963.

[3] Productivity within a single sector may be compared between regions or time periods in physical terms, bushels of wheat per man employed, or per acre, etc. This chapter is concerned exclusively with productivity comparisons between sectors in which income stands as the measure of how much is produced.

[4] The most frequently cited source of productivity statistics is S. Kuznets, 'Quantitative Aspects of the Economic Growth of Nations Part II', *Economic Development and Cultural Change*, July 1957, Table 5.

exactly as we have computed ratio of agricultural to non-agricultural productivity in Thailand in the introduction to Part III.

In this chapter we alter the productivity statistics to make them fit the context of the debate about tariff policy. The statistics are cited as evidence of a misallocation of resources. The ideal statistics would therefore show all industries to be equally productive when nothing would be gained by moving labour from one industry to another. Two qualifications are needed. First, the ideal statistics would attribute different productivities to industries using different amounts of capital or of land per unit of labour. Second, allowance would have to be made for skill differentials in the wage structure. Industries using highly skilled and expensive labour would have high productivities that would not be evidence of a misallocation of the labour force.

There are, however, four other ways in which the usual productivity measures might attribute unequal productivities in the absence of a misallocation of the labour force; two of these are associated with links in the chain of prices and two are of a more statistical nature outside our main concern.

(1) Statistics of national income of underdeveloped countries may contain errors of measurement. Value added in agriculture may exclude some subsistence farming. Value added in manufacturing, usually estimated from tax data, is underestimated whenever income is not reported in the tax returns. Value added in trade and distribution is particularly subject to error; frequently the absence of reliable data on this sector, forces statisticians to estimate its share of income by imposing a 'reasonable' mark up on other items in the national accounts.

(2) The usual method of compiling productivity statistics fails to make allowance for the distinction between the farming industry and farmers as a social class. The productivity of agriculture is computed by dividing the value added of farm products by the agricultural labour force. But farmers do more than grow food. They build and care for their own houses, invest in rural improvements, and work at cottage industry or in the cities in the off-seasons. The value added attributed to farmers as a social class ought to account for the products of these other activities along with the purely agricultural output.

(3) A difference in income per man employed between agriculture and other sectors is not necessarily indicative of a differences in

living standards because the income differential may be balanced by a comparable differential in the price levels facing people in these sectors. A farmer is not worse off than a city dweller if the farmer's lower income is accompanied by a lower price level. The examples of Chapter 10 have shown how differences among sectors in money income can coexist with identical real incomes and an optimal distribution of the labour force. Productivity statistics can be corrected for price levels facing workers in different industries so that a residual difference in productivity is evidence of misallocation.

(4) The demonstration in Chapter 11 that the tax structure normally influences statistics of income per man employed by industry does not carry the implication that these statistics should always be adjusted for the effects of the tax system. Income per man employed as an indication of income distribution among social classes obviously requires no modification to compensate for the effects of the tax system, because it is irrelevant in this usage of the statistics why incomes are high or low. But statistics of income per man employed should be adjusted to compensate for the influence of the tax system when these statistics serve as measures of productivity used in deciding whether a tariff is required, for the tariff must be justified with reference to economic conditions as they would be without the tariff. International transport cost does not bias the productivity statistics because the allocation of factors of production among industries in any country is established in response to world prices, f.o.b. for exports or c.i.f. for imports, at the home port.

In this chapter we try to assess the orders of magnitude of these four biases in the productivity figures, and to show how the conventional statistics might be corrected. The example chosen is the ratio of agricultural productivity to productivity in the rest of the economy in Thailand in 1963. We begin by measuring this ratio in the usual way, and go on to adjust it to correct for each of the biases in turn. Alternative measures of productivity are summarized in Table 21. The top row shows productivity figures constructed in the usual way. The other rows show these figures altered to include the full income of farmers under agriculture, to adjust for price levels, to compensate for the effects of the tax system, and to correct for an alleged error in the measurement of income. The corrections cumulate down the rows so that the bottom row includes them all.

The result of these corrections is to raise the ratio of farm to non-farm income per worker from about a tenth to about a third. It will be evident on examining the details of these corrections that the estimates of bias are themselves subject to a wide range of error. What is established by the figures is that the combined magnitude of the four biases in the productivity figures is to be assessed, not in percentage points, but in hundreds of per cent.

TABLE 21

Alternative Comparisons of Income Per Man Employed 1963

	Agriculture (baht)	Other sectors (baht)	Ratio (%)
Calculations based on national income accounting	1675	16 764	10
Corrected to include all the income of farmers under agriculture	2579	14 287	18
Corrected additionally for differences in cost of living	3070	14 287	21
Corrected additionally for the effects of the tax system	4014	13 703	29
Corrected additionally for presumed over-valuation of income in trade	4014	11 558	35

Biases in productivity statistics that are similar in kind, but not necessarily in magnitude or even direction, are probably to be found for other underdeveloped countries. Thailand's productivity statistics are atypical of the underdeveloped countries as a whole in that the ratio of Thai agricultural to non-agricultural productivity is almost at the bottom of the list. This, combined with the fact that Thailand is a large-scale exporter of agricultural products, would lead one to think that the statistical bias against agriculture is greater in Thailand than elsewhere. The understatement of farm income and the difference in rural and urban costs of living, probably have their counterparts in other underdeveloped countries. The last two corrections could go either way. An import tax on food would bias up the income of farmers, and little can be said *a priori* about the effects of measurement errors.

(a) CORRECTIONS TO INCLUDE ALL THE OUTPUT OF FARMERS UNDER AGRICULTURE

The ideal measure of the productivity of farmers ought to take account of the full earnings of the farmers, including earnings associated with non-agricultural pursuits. The usual measure of farmers' income, as calculated above, falls short of this ideal, both by failing to record the farmers' earnings over and above sales of crops as part of his income and by attributing this income to other sectors.

(1) The usual method of computing agricultural income attributes the imputed rents of rural dwellings to the non-farm sector because this item is not recorded in the accounts under agriculture. Obviously, if rents of urban dwellings are to be included as part of non-farm income, then rents of rural dwellings ought to be included as part of farmers' income. Transferring this item from non-farm to farm income reduces the former and increases the latter by 2007 million baht.[1]

(2) Value added in construction attributable to the building of farm houses, the opening of new lands, and the making of farm tools by farmers, should be counted as farm rather than non-farm income. The sum of these items is 1269 million baht.

(3) Farmers engage in non-agricultural activities such as making cloth and weaving baskets, and many people who are primarily farmers work outside the agricultural sector, either in manufacturing or in trade, for part of the year. There is no official estimate of income of farmers from these sources. For the want of anything better, I guess that the typical farmer works

---

[1] All figures referring to the Thai National Accounts are either taken from the published accounts or furnished by the Thai National Income Office.

one month at non-farm occupations for which he earns 300 baht. This adds an extra 3204 million baht to farm income.[1]

The total farm income (million baht) is therefore:

agricultural crops	18 419
livestock	2007
ownership of homes	2504
construction (i.e. new lands, local production of houses and tools)	1269
work outside the farm sector	3204
Total	27 403

The measure of the farm labour force might also be adjusted. It appears from the numbers of men and women in the labour force statistics that most women of the appropriate age group living on farms are recorded in the statistics as farm workers. Since these women must spend some of their time in housework, it seems reasonable to suppose that they are less than full-time farmers. Consequently we suppose the effective size of the female agricultural labour force to be three quarters of the number recorded in the census. This reduces the total farm labour force to 10 635 thousand.[2]

These corrections bring income per man employed on farms up to 2577,[3] and income per man employed in the rest of the economy down to 14 289,[4] raising the ratio of farm to non-farm income per man employed from 10 to 18 per cent.

(b) DIFFERENCES IN THE COST OF LIVING BETWEEN RURAL AND URBAN AREAS

Only a small part of the remaining income differential can be attributed to differences in the cost of living. There are no statistics of rural and urban cost of living in Thailand, but a difference in

---

[1] The effective agricultural labour force is estimated below to be 10 635 thousand people. The product of 300 and 10 680 thousand is 3204 million.

[2] In 1960 there were 5·47 million men and 5·72 million women in the agricultural labour force. The original estimate of the total farm labour force in 1963 is 12 194 thousand workers, the sum of the male and female labour force in 1960 scaled up by 9%.

[3] 27 403/10 635 thousand.

[4] (67 650–27 403)/2817 thousand.

living costs can be estimated in a rough way from transport and distribution costs, for prices of similar goods cannot differ between two places by more than the cost of bringing them from one place to the other.

Consider first the transport and distribution cost of rice. Taking the average distance between rice farms and Bangkok to be about 200 kilometres, and trucks to be the typical means of transport, we see that the average percentage difference in rice prices

TABLE 22

Thai Transport Cost: Kilograms of Rice per Ton Kilometre

canal boat (long haul, 400 km.)	0·07
truck (long haul, 400–700 km)	0·15
rail (long haul, 400–700 km)	0·15
truck (short haul, miller's discounts for collecting paddy at farms)	1·0
ox-cart (used only for carrying small quantities short distances)	2·5

Source: Approximate figures based on graph 2, Chapter III, and an assumed rice price of 1·5 baht a kilogramme.

between farms and cities attributable to transport cost alone is only 3 per cent.[1] Transport alone does not impose a significantly large bias on the productivity statistics.[2]

A somewhat larger difference between urban and rural rice prices arises when distribution cost as well as transport cost is taken into

[1] It costs 0·15 × 200 kilograms or 0·03 tons of rice to bring one ton from the farms to Bangkok.

[2] Present-day instances can be found in which geographical price differentials due to transport cost are important. For instance, rice was carried by coolies for 200 kilometres over mountains to supply the Vietnamese attackers at Dien Bien Phu. Of the amount initially dispatched, nine-tenths had to be consumed by the coolies themselves en route. Had a national income been computed for North Vietnam and Laos at that time, it would have contained a tenfold equalizing component between Dien Bien Phu and the coast. There would have been a fivefold differential between rural and urban rice prices in Thailand if rice had to be transported by ox-cart instead of by truck.

account. The typical pattern of transport, processing, and distribution cost described in Table 19 attributes 79 per cent of the Thai retail price to farmers and 21 per cent to millers and traders of all kinds. Not all of the 21 per cent represents a gap between the prices of rice in the city and on the farms. The middleman's mark-up and the milling cost must be incurred wherever rice is consumed. Only transport and retail mark-up, amounting to 16 per cent of the farm price, represents a genuine difference in rural and urban cost.

Other mark-ups are shown in Table 23.

TABLE 23

Estimates of gross Mark-ups in Thailand

retailers of fruit and vegetables	20–30%
retailers of pork and beef	5–10%
commission agents (rice)	$\frac{1}{2}$%
wholesalers of agricultural products	5–10%
exporters of rice and jute (exclusive of the export tax)	$\frac{1}{3}$–$\frac{1}{2}$%
buyers of farm products	2–5%

Source: These statistics were obtained from interviews with traders.

Differences between the prices paid by farmers and city people for other food crops would appear to be smaller than that for rice because the farmer tends to buy most of his food, other than rice, at local markets where retail mark-ups are as high as those in the city. Thus, the main difference between urban and rural price levels of farm products other than rice consists of transport, spoilage, and wholesaler's cost. Transport cost is perhaps a bit higher on other food products than on rice and the wholesaler's mark-up is, as shown in Table 23, usually between 5 and 10 per cent.

Differences in urban and rural prices of goods shipped from the city to the farm tend to be smaller yet. Many wholesalers of products imported for local consumption arrange to keep prices uniform over the country. Also, transport cost usually represents a small proportion of the value of such products because of their large value per unit of weight.

My guess is that the average difference between rural and urban price levels for transportable products is about 10 per cent, 20 per cent at the outside, and not nearly enough to have a major effect on the meaning of the statistics of income per man employed.

Housing is an additional source of divergence between urban and rural costs of living. The national accounts impute rents of 1200 and 600 baht per annum on the lowest class of urban dwellings and average farm houses. At least half of the former figure represents site rent. We raise the imputed rent of farm-houses from 600 to 1200 baht, in the belief that a typical farm-house is at least as comfortable as the sort of urban dwelling that could be got for 1200 baht rent per annum. This adds another 2504 million baht to farm income.

Corrections for these differences between rural and urban costs of living, raise farm income to 32 647 million[1] and income per man employed to 3070 baht per annum. The proportion of farm to non-farm income per man employed rises from 18 to 21 per cent.

(c) THE EFFECTS OF THE TAX SYSTEM

We now attempt to estimate the incomes of farmers and other social classes as they would appear in the accounts if the present tax structure, consisting largely of trade taxes and other indirect taxes, were replaced by an income tax.

As stated in Part II, Chapter 11, the reasons for choosing an income tax as the basis of comparison are that this tax ensures that domestic prices differ from world prices by not more than transport and distribution cost, and that the private revenue equals the social product of each factor of production. An export tax puts a gap between social product and private return in the export industry. A sales tax makes the output of the industry on which it is levied appear larger than is necessary to get factors of production to enter that industry. In assessing the Thai distribution of income as it would be if all revenue were raised through an income tax, we begin by showing how the export tax on rice reduces the farmers' income, and then go on to show how other taxes increase value added in manufacturing and trade.

[1] $(27\ 403 \times 1 \cdot 10) + 2504.$

The export tax on rice is about 90 per cent of the farm price. Allowing for a 3 per cent fall in the world price of rice,[1] and supposing that distribution margins remain unchanged, the abolition of the tax on the export of rice would increase the Thai farm price by 85 per cent. As rice constitutes about half the value of agricultural crops in the national income, the immediate effect of the abolition of the export tax on rice is to increase value added in agricultural crops by about 40 per cent. There is an additional effect, due to substitutability between rice and other crops. It is useful to think of three types of agricultural products: rice, other exported crops, and agricultural products consumed at home and not exported. If the export tax on rice were abolished, the domestic price of rice would increase. Prices of other exported agricultural products would not change because these prices are set in world markets. Prices of agricultural products that do not enter international trade would probably increase, but by a smaller percentage than the increase in the price of rice, for agricultural products that do not enter into international trade are substitutes

---

[1] Rice is the only commodity for which Thai exports contribute a significantly large share of the world market. Consequently we suppose that world prices of commodities other than rice are fixed independently of the volume of Thai trade. To estimate the effect on the world price of the abolition of the Thai export tax on rice, we suppose elasticities of demand for and supply of rice to be the same in Thailand and in the rest of the world. The abolition of the export tax raises the domestic price of rice; the surplus available for export increases both because production increases and because domestic demand is reduced; the extra rice offered for sale on the world market causes the world price to decrease. Our assumption about equal elasticities in Thailand and elsewhere, implies that the percentage changes in the Thai price of rice and in the world price of rice are both proportional to the percentage changes in total supplies of rice to be consumed (and not merely traded) in these two markets. Thailand's share of world rice output is just over 3 per cent. A given amount of extra Thai exports therefore represents a percentage change in world rice supply of only 3 per cent of the percentage change in Thai rice supply, and there is a corresponding effect on prices.

The abolition of the export tax on rice may affect the productivity of rice farming in reality and not just in appearance. There may be a change in real output per man employed due to a shift along the production function. The direction of change cannot be ascertained *a priori*. An increase in the output of rice due to an increase of the proportion of the labour force engaged in rice cultivation would tend to lower productivity of labour. But many agricultural economists in Thailand claim that the abolition of the export tax on rice would exert its major effect on the total output of rice by lowering the relative price of fertilizer in terms of rice and thereby expanding fertilizer use. If this view is correct, the productivity of labour in rice production would increase when the domestic price of rice increases.

in production and in use, both for rice and for other exported agricultural products. To place a figure on the net effect of the abolition of the export tax on the prices of agricultural products that do not enter into international trade, we supposed that the pull on the price of untraded agricultural commodities of the different export crops is proportional to their values in export; as rice constitutes 62 per cent of the value of exports of agricultural products, we suppose that the value of domestically consumed crops rises 62 per cent of the rise in the rice price, i.e. by 53 per cent. The net effect of these price changes[1] is to increase the gross domestic product of agriculture by 10 044 million baht, from 32 647 million baht to 42 691 million baht.

It is difficult to assess the effect of the tariff on income in manufacturing. One can cite industries where the tariff buoys up the value added considerably. The automobile assembly industry in Thailand, as in many other countries, is a case in point. There is a 60 per cent tariff on finished automobiles and a 30 per cent tariff on completely-knocked-down automobiles. As the cost c.i.f. of all imported parts is about 9/10 of the cost c.i.f. of the completed automobile, the effective rate of protection on the process of assembly is 300 per cent; under present tax arrangements it pays a firm to assemble cars in Thailand if it can be done at less than three times the cost of assembly abroad. Value added in car assembly at world prices may well be negative, even though the industry is very profitable at local prices.[2]

The net effect of the tariffs taken as a whole is not necessarily to protect Thai manufacturing because a large portion of the tariff is levied on products not made in Thailand or on industrial raw material, particularly petroleum products. It may be that the protective effect of the tariff on a few manufactures competing with exports is over-balanced by its disprotective effect on other types

---

[1] The value added of rice production rises 85 per cent, from 9041 to 16 726 million baht. The value added of other exported agricultural products, including rubber, livestock, jute, maize, etc., remains unchanged at 9197 million baht. The value added of agricultural products not exported, including fruit, vegetables, poultry, eggs and pigs, rises 53 per cent from 5206 to 7965 million baht.

[2] The effective rate of protection on an industrial process is the percentage by which the value added is increased by the tax system. The value added in assembly is the difference between the cost of the parts and the cost of the complete car. The tax system increased this gap by 30 per cent of the value of the complete car which is 300 per cent of the value added in the process of assembly.

of manufactures.[1] We are therefore supposing that the tariff causes no net change in the measure of value added of industries other than agriculture, for the net effect of the tariff could go either way.

A number of indirect taxes are levied primarily on the trade and manufacturing sectors. These are:

business and stamp tax	1797
selective sales tax	1072
automobile tax	103
revenue of the tobacco monopoly	320
Total	3292

There is some question as to whether these taxes ought to be deducted from income, for the correct procedure in accordance with our programme of estimating the incomes when all indirect taxes and trade taxes are replaced by an income tax, is to deduct only taxes that are shifted forward. The removal of an indirect tax on a single commodity normally causes the price of the commodity to fall by the amount of tax removed, for the extra income tax, required to maintain the total public revenue, is levied on the whole community and affects producers of this commodity to an insignificant extent. The more commodities involved, the more is the fall in their price checked by the income tax; the replacement of a general sales tax on all commodities by an income tax, need not cause any fall in the general price level. In Thailand, indirect taxes yield a fairly large proportion of the total revenue and the burden of an extra income tax caused by the removal of all indirect taxes might fall heavily on the commercial classes who now pay the indirect tax. We shall suppose that the removal of the indirect taxes would cause a fall in the values of the commodities on which they are imposed equal to half the tax revenue; we therefore deduct half the revenue of these taxes from the income of the non-farm sector, decreasing the income of this sector from 40 247 million to 38 601 million baht.

[1] This dual effect of the tariff structure is not accidental. It corresponds to the Thai policy of encouraging new types of industries and discouraging the establishment of additional firms in old types of industries. Automobile assembly represents one extreme; at the other extreme is the fact that as a rule licenses are no longer granted for the construction of new rice mills.

The net effect of the Thai tax system on the distribution of income is to reduce the income of farmers. A tax system need not have this effect, and the net effect in many countries is in the opposite direction. Yet there is a strong economic reason why the tax system works this way in Thailand. In Thailand, as in many under-developed countries where direct taxes on farmers are exceedingly costly to collect, the tax system is oriented toward trade taxes and direct taxes on other social classes. The role of the export tax is to place a tax burden on the farmer indirectly. He himself pays almost no tax. But the low price of food caused by the export tax is like a subsidy from the farmer to other social classes, which are then taxed directly in a variety of ways. The picture of a farmer with low productivity and who pays no tax gives way on analysis to a picture of a farmer with a higher productivity who is, in fact, taxed quite heavily in a round-about way.

(d) THE MEASUREMENT OF INCOME

One of the by-products of the chain of prices in Tables 18–20 and of the data on traders' mark-ups in Table 23, is a check on the estimate of value added in trade and distribution in the national accounts. The estimate in the accounts is got by what is called the commodity-flow method; a fixed percentage mark-up is added to other items in the accounts and to imports. The percentages are as follows:

imports	30%
agriculture	20%
livestock	16%
fish	5%
minerals	13%
manufacturing	52%

These percentages are of value added by industry inclusive of the portion of the produce that is not traded at all, inclusive of food grown and consumed on the farm and of manufactures sold directly by the manufacturer to the customer. The commodity-flow method of estimating value added in trade is, of course, used as a last resort because statistics of value added of retailers and wholesalers are not as yet (1965) available. The percentages represent little more than educated guesses about conventional mark-ups. Comparing these percentages with those of Table 23, it appears that the estimate of value added in trade in the accounts is much too high. I guess that value added in trade in the accounts is twice what it ought to be. Deducting half of the value added in trade from non-agricultural income, reduces non-agricultural income to 32 559 million baht, or 11 558 baht per annum per man employed.

(e) POSSIBLE CAUSES OF THE REMAINING DIFFERENCE BETWEEN THE PRODUCTIVITY OF AGRICULTURE AND OF OTHER SECTORS

Corrections to the productivity figures, summarized in Table 21, increase the ratio of the productivity of agriculture to the productivity of other sectors from a tenth to a third. A threefold difference in productivity among sectors still seems quite large, and it is interesting to speculate on possible causes. Several explanations present themselves. Differences between farm and non-farm incomes may be caused by differences in amounts of co-operating factors of production, by skill differentials in the wage structure, by non-pecuniary advantages to employment in agriculture, or by imperfections in the labour market such as irrationality of farmers in refusing to take up high-paying jobs in the city.

Differences in amounts of co-operating factors may not be very significant. The co-operating factor of production in agriculture is, of course, land. Rents on agriculture land usually vary between 20 and 50 per cent of the crop. If we suppose the average rent to be 35 per cent, the share of income accruing to non-human factors of production in Thai agriculture would not be significantly different from the share of non-human factors of production in the national product of the United Kingdom,[1] and it seems reasonable to suppose that the share of non-human factors of production is about the same in the non-agricultural sector of Thailand as in the U.K. as a whole. Labour is relatively cheap in Thailand, but industrial production tends to be labour intensive and the non-farm sector includes elements like medicine and public administration that are almost pure labour. It seems unlikely that a major part of the threefold difference in productivity could be explained by differing labour shares in the income of the farm and non-farm

[1] In 1963 the ratio of 'total income from employment' to 'gross national product' in the U.K. was 67 per cent (Table I, *National Income and Expenditure 1965*, H.M.S.O.).

sectors. It is even possible that the share of non-human factors is greater in agriculture.

There remain as explanations skill differentials in the wage structure, non-pecuniary advantages to employment in agriculture, and irrationality or other imperfections in the labour market. Though it is very difficult to distinguish among these explanations, some evidence on this issue can be got by examining the wage structure. A large gap between all farm wages and all non-farm wages would suggest a barrier that farmers are unwilling or unable to cross. A gap between wages of unskilled labour on farms and in cities no larger than might be explained by the higher cost of living (especially housing) in the city would suggest the absence of large-scale misallocation in the labour market.

TABLE 24

Wages in Thailand (baht per day)

unskilled farm labour—Northern Thailand	6
unskilled farm labour—Central Plain	10
unskilled farm labour—piece work at harvest— Central Plain	20
driver of bicycle taxi—in the City	15–20
unskilled workers in rice mills, factories or repairing roads	10–15
earnings of small retail trader of fruit, vegetables, meat, etc.	20–50
skilled blacksmith, coolie (at wharf), forest worker, machinist, fisherman	50
graduate engineer or shorthand-typist in English	100–200

Source: Interviews.

A sample of wages in Table 24 suggests something of a continuity between rural and urban wages. A farm worker living near Bangkok cannot improve his position very much by working in the city unless he is skilled, for the lowest of the urban wages are not higher than the typical farm wage and farm wages at harvest time are above wages of unskilled workers in small factories. Differentials among skills seem large enough to account for a threefold differential between farm and non-farm income per worker, for most of the high-paying jobs are in the non-farm sector and the skill of the farmer is so widespread that it commands no premium.

This evidence is not strong enough to rule out altogether the possibility of explaining income differentials between farms and other sectors by irrationality or market imperfections. But it lends some plausibility to an alternative explanation which, if true, would allow the income statistics no place in the argument justifying tariffs or other assistance to manufactures in compensation for conservatism of people in choosing jobs.

List of Symbols

Income

Y national income in local currency.

$Y^{\$}$ national income in dollars calculated by dividing Y by the foreign exchange rate.

$Y_{T\pounds}$ national income per head of Thailand valued at U.K. prices in $\pounds$.

$Y_{U\text{baht}}$, $Y_{U\pounds}$, $Y_{T\text{baht}}$ are defined analogously to $Y_{T\pounds}$.

Y_{TU} national income per head of Thailand valued in units or machines (or in units of 'goods' in Chapter 8) at U.K. relative prices.

Y_{UT}, Y_{TT}, Y_{UU} are defined analogously to Y_{TU}.

$Y_{UT'}$ national income of the U.K. assessed by Thai standards. $Y_{TU'}$ is defined analogously to $Y_{UT'}$.

Y_F, Y_T, Y_S, Y_C total income accruing to farm workers, transport workers, landlords, civil servants.

Y_U, Y_T (in Chapter 9), incomes of the U.K. and Thailand in units of bundles of goods of equal value in both countries.

Prices and quantities

P_{iT} price of the good i in Thailand.

P_{GT}, P_{MT}, P_{ST}, P_{iU}, P_{GU}, P_{MU}, P_{SU} prices where G, M, and S in the first subscript refers to grain (except in Chapter 8, where G refers to 'goods') machines, or services, and where U in the second subscript refers to the U.K.

Q_{iT} quantity per head of the good i consumed in Thailand.

Q_{GT}, Q_{MT}, Q_{ST}, Q_{iU}, Q_{GU}, Q_{MU}, Q_{SU} quantities per head with subscripts the same as for prices.

Q_M, Q_G, $\overline{Q}_M$, $\overline{Q}_G$ specific quantities of machines and grain.

$P(D)$ the price of grain at D.

$P_i(D)$, $Q_i(D)$ price and quantity of the good i at location D.

P_I, P_E prices of imports and exports in the local currency.

$P_I^\$$, $P_E^\$$ prices of imports and exports in U.S. dollars.

$P_i^\$$ price of the good i in U.S. dollars.

P_U, P_T ratios of the purchasing power of money in Thailand and the U.K.

Other terms

a_{ij} input–output coefficient.

C consumption of grain per head.

D, $\overline{D}$ locations. Some variables are functions of D.

D^* radius of a disc-shaped country.

$\hat{D}$ the optimum location.

E efficiency term in a Cobb–Douglas production function.

F foreign exchange rate.

G total output of grain.

G_F, G_T, G_S, G_C, G_M total consumption of grain of the social classes: farm workers, transport workers, landlords, civil servants, and workers making machines.

g a subscript referring to gross (as opposed to net).

l number of farm workers per unit area.

L labour force.

L_F, L_T, L_M, L_C labour force engaged as farm workers, transport workers, workers making machines, and civil servants.

n a subscript referring to net (as opposed to gross).

N_U, N_F, N_T lines on Fig. 11.

O output of grain per unit area.

R_T, R_U production possibility curves in Thailand and the U.K.

S number of landowners.

T, T', $\overline{T}$ indicate consumption patterns.

T transport cost of grain measured as tons of grain per ton kilometre. (This definition is generalized in the appendices of Chapter 10.)

T_i, T_G, T_M percentage appreciation of the prices of good i, of grain, and of machines due to transport cost.

t, t_i rate of tax($+$), tariff($+$), or subsidy($-$) on the good i. (The subscript is used when more than one good is discussed.)

U, U', $\overline{U}$ indicate consumption patterns.

$U(Q_1 \ldots Q_N)$ a utility function.

U_i the marginal utility of the good i.

U_1, U_2 indifference curves.

W, W_1, W_2, W_3 wages in grain.

$W(D)$ wage in money at D.

$Z_G(D)$ an amount of grain transported from farms to the city.

α exponent representing labour's share of the product in the Cobb–Douglas production function.

β, β_G transport cost of grain measured in man-years per ton kilometre.

β_M transport cost of machines.

$\mu(D)$ marginal utility of income.

γ number of machines consumed per ton of grain.

δ output of machines per worker.

Δ increment.

d derivative.